EXTRAORDINARY

Hospitality

for ORDINARY CHRISTIANS

EXTRAORDINARY
Hospitality
for ORDINARY CHRISTIANS

A Radical Approach to Preparing Your Heart & Home for Gospel-Centered Community

Victoria Duerstock

Good Books
New York, New York

Good Books books may be purchased in bulk at special discounts for sales promotion, corporate gifts, fund-raising, or educational purposes. Special editions can also be created to specifications. For details, contact the Special Sales Department, Good Books, 307 West 36th Street, 11th Floor, New York, NY 10018 or info@skyhorsepublishing.com.

Good Books is an imprint of Skyhorse Publishing, Inc.®, a Delaware corporation.

Visit our website at www.goodbooks.com.

10 9 8 7 6 5 4 3 2 1

Library of Congress Cataloging-in-Publication Data is available on file.

ISBN: 978-1-68099-618-0
eBook ISBN: 978-1-68099-680-7

Cover design by Mona Lin
Cover photo by Caroline Bivens, @c.b._designs/www.carolinebivensdesigns.com

Printed in China

Contents

INTRODUCTION	VII
WHAT IS BIBLICAL HOSPITALITY?	**1**
EARLY CHURCH EXAMPLE	1
SPACE FOR THE SPIRIT TO MOVE	2
LETTING GO OF PERFECTION	4
A MISSIONAL HOME	6
MOVING THE ROADBLOCKS	19
OTHER BIBLICAL EXAMPLES	21
ENTERTAINMENT VS. HOSPITALITY	27
A RIGHT ATTITUDE	31
TASTE AND SEE	32
DISASTERS AND OPPORTUNITIES	34
LOVING MY NEIGHBOR	36
DECLUTTERING	**39**
WHY IS CLUTTER A PROBLEM?	41
LESS IS MORE	43
CLEAR IT OUT	44
HOW MUCH IS ENOUGH?	47
A DECLUTTERED MIND	51
A DECLUTTERED HEART	52
BEING INTENTIONAL	55
CHOOSING COMFORT AND CARE	59
PRACTICAL DECLUTTERING TIPS	62
DECLUTTERING THE WHOLE HOME	66
CLEANING TIPS & TRICKS	**69**
UNITY, HARMONY, AND CLEANLINESS	69
WORK IS MESSY	70
CREATING GOOD HABITS	74
WHEN SHOULD I HIRE HELP?	79
CLEANING TIPS & HACKS	79
MEAL PLANNING & MENUS	**85**
AFTERNOON OR EVENING SNACKS	86
WHIP-IT-UP QUICK RECIPES	88
PARTY FOOD & SMALL BITES	91
SANDWICH FILLERS	94
SALADS	96
MUFFINS & BREAKFAST	99
MAKE AHEAD & FREEZE	102
MAIN DISHES	104
SIDE DISHES	111
BARS & COOKIES	113
CAKES & PIES	118
HANDY SUBSTITUTIONS	124
MENU PLANNING	126
START WITH WHAT YOU HAVE	128
ADDITIONAL THOUGHTS	**135**
PREPARING FOR OVERNIGHT GUESTS	135
HYGGE AND *FIKA*	136
FLOW	140
STYLE	143
FORM & FUNCTION	147
CROSS-CULTURAL HOSPITALITY	151
MODELING HOSPITALITY	152
BIBLICAL HOSPITALITY IS COUNTERCULTURAL	152
IN OUR COMMUNITY AND THE WORLD	156
ENDNOTES	**158**
PHOTOGRAPHY CREDITS	**159**

Introduction

As Christ followers, we sometimes forget the power of an open door to a lost world. Using our homes as a missional extension of living out our faith in the true model of the Great Commission might be challenging in our fast-paced, nonstop lives, but it's not impossible. As with anything though, if our hearts are not in the right place, we will struggle with having the right perspective and priorities for the gifts we've been given. Having a home that is always open and available is key to living in community with others and being missional in our thinking.

Instead of feeling that our homes should be immaculate or professionally decorated before we allow neighbors and strangers in, what if we could learn to be honest with others about our lived-in spaces and bring them in to our homes anyway, to live life together? In the pages that follow, you will find practical living tips to help you feel more confident in keeping your home available to others. My prayer is that you will find encouragement and inspiration to let the Holy Spirit overflow from your heart into your home and out into your community. Letting our guard down and opening our doors to connect with people allows us to love others as Jesus did.

What Is Biblical Hospitality?

Love is not an abstract theory we only talk about, but a way of life demonstrated through our loving deeds.

—Larry Dugger

Early Church Example

And they continued stedfastly in the apostles' doctrine and fellowship, and in breaking of bread, and in prayers. And fear came upon every soul: and many wonders and signs were done by the apostles. And all that believed were together, and had all things common; And sold their possessions and goods, and parted them to all men, as every man had need. And they, continuing daily with one accord in the temple, and breaking bread from house to house, did eat their meat with gladness and singleness of heart, Praising God, and having favour with all the people. And the Lord added to the church daily such as should be saved. Acts 2:42–47

This passage clearly teaches us that the fellowship that the early church believers devoted themselves to included the teaching of the apostles, gathering together and breaking bread, and praying. They lived life together, sharing where one had a need, watching God move in their midst, and praising Him daily. They received and shared their meals alongside one another, and the Lord grew their numbers as they lived in this manner through souls being saved and lives changed.

While this early model can't quite be replicated in our society today, we can at least be more intentional with how and where we spend our resources. When I say resources, I'm not just speaking of money, but also of our time and energy and talents. My heart's passion is for each of us to look beyond the living of this daily life in the messy here and now, and live life for the kingdom.

Space for the Spirit to Move

Kingdom living requires a view of the future. It requires creating space for God to move and for me to slow. It's ironic that with all the technology and advancements we have seen through the years, we have not actually slowed down. We are not content to achieve the same amount of work in less time. Rather, we have inverted that concept and declared that every available amount of time needs to be squeezed and wrung out to its maximum capability. And herein lies the problem. When we pack the schedule so tight there's no room to breathe, and add to the to-do list faster than we check things off, we eventually break down under the pressure.

It's sad really, but we've managed to reduce our lives to a series of objectives. When we occasionally find success, we wonder what's next. We ask, what should I do with myself now? Scary, right?

What if, instead, we were to create enough margin—space, really—in our schedules, our hearts, and our homes that if a friend called and had a need, we could easily shut down what we are doing and could go take care of it. If someone called and needed prayer, we wouldn't

worry about the interruption to our schedules, but would rather be grateful for the opportunity to take a friend before the throne of God.

What if, friends, we were to shift our priorities so that we spend a morning just deep diving into God's word, meditating, reading and memorizing what He has to say to us and then praying for those we know need healing, restoration, and divine intervention?

Wouldn't our lives look and feel different?

Moses came away from the presence of God with a glow about Him. People *knew* he had been with God, and he didn't have to say a word. Seriously, read more in Exodus 34 and let the word impact you with the fact that Moses had to cover his face because he was literally shining from having been in the presence of God!

It may feel like you are a victim of your own schedule and that you are just trying to survive the demands put on you, the kids' activities, and the work required to pay the bills. But you probably have more choice about how you spend your time than you think. The first step may be taking a moment to stop worrying about everything you think you have to do today, and instead consider all that God has blessed you with, all the ways He has provided above and beyond your needs.

You might not feel abundantly blessed today, but can I pose the following observation? If you are reading this book, whether in print form or on an e-reader, you are abundantly blessed. So many people around the world don't have the luxury of time or resources to afford to be able to do even such a simple thing as reading a book.

Lest you feel like I'm preaching at you, please know that this is something I wrestle with *all the time*. I deal with the natural pressures to do more, be more, get more done on a daily basis. The only thing that brings me back to the true desires I have for myself, my family, my home, and my neighbors is the time I spend—really spend—alone with God each day. It changes everything about me, especially the way that I think. Whatever you do, don't cut your time with God. It's essential. It's life-giving. It changes everything. So start with prioritizing time alone with God and noticing the abundance of what God has given you.

> Whatever you do, don't cut your time with God. It's essential. It's life-giving. It changes everything.

Letting Go of Perfection

The next hurdle, at least for me, is overcoming perfectionism. I don't like to do anything until I know I can do it perfectly. Anyone else?

Thanks to perfectionism, I have the gift of procrastination. Except it's really not a gift. It's the opposite, and it paralyzes any good intentions from ever becoming action. It paralyzes me, because when I look at a task that needs doing, I want to be all in and get it all done. This means that if I only have ten or fifteen minutes to get something done but I think it will take me an hour, I am not even going to start. The same holds true with inviting friends, neighbors, or especially strangers over. If I don't have time to clean the house from top to bottom and inside to outside, then I won't extend the invitation. I feel like I don't have time to be a perfect host in a perfectly neat and clean home, so I don't want to do it all.

I was recently challenged to consider that if something is worth doing, it's worth doing badly. To be fair, my first reaction was quite negative. I bristled pretty hard at this concept because it flies in the face of doing all things well. What about Colossians 3:23: "And whatsoever ye do, do it heartily, as to the Lord, and not unto men"? I've always believed that meant I should present my very best efforts to God in all things. But I sat and listened a little while longer. We were at a newly formed board meeting for a nonprofit and the chairman shared these thoughts. As much as we want to do things "right" or "perfectly," sometimes we must instead act with the information we have today and do the best we can or know how to do in that moment. Because if we wait for the perfect time, or the perfect way, we will wait forever, and nothing will get done. Maybe that Bible verse is more about our heart posture—about having our hearts in the right place in whatever we're doing—than about perfection. I really sat with this concept long after this meeting was over, and I can tell you it is so impactful for me to remember this lesson. It's really what I'm saying to you here today.

> If we wait for the perfect time, or the perfect way, we will wait forever, and nothing will get done.

- Do it anyway, whether you have it figured out or not.
- Do it anyway, whether you have all the space you need or not.
- Do it anyway, whether you can make a five-course meal or not.
- Do it anyway, whether you have matching dishes, glasses, and dinnerware or not.

A Missional Home

Biblical hospitality doesn't require anything from us beyond a willingness to take anything that God has given us and present it as available for someone else. It requires an obedient heart and a willing spirit. It requires sacrificing time and energy for someone else. But the rewards, my friend, are so sweet. God provides magnificently when we start to take those steps of obedience. When we long to bring Him all the glory and praise, He rewards us immeasurably with just what we need for that day. He brings us new friends and gives us the opportunity to share a Gospel conversation with someone who just might need to hear about the goodness of God that leads men to repentance. There's no joy like the joy of leading someone to the Lord.

But we have to position ourselves to be obedient. That's why this book exists. Let's declutter, clean, make a meal, and prepare our hearts, but let's not wait until we have it all done perfectly to say "Yes" to God. Let's not wait to invite our neighbors over for a cup of coffee, a tea party, or even breakfast.

We've had so much fun entertaining in the past by hosting breakfast on a Saturday.

Throw some pancakes, maple syrup, and OJ out and enjoy a slow morning together. Breakfast doesn't take forever to prepare,

the ingredients are pretty inexpensive, and no one is awake enough to care how clean or unclean your home is. Starting small and simple is the best way to lay the foundation for a habit of hospitality.

Having a heart that is in tune with the Father's heart requires us to pursue His word and apply its truths. As we consistently, daily, show up and do the work, He fills us with His power and grace to see others as He sees them in our homes. We must see even our families in light of His grace. Our service to them in the daily laundry piles, breakfast making, and cleaning can easily become dull and dreary if we are not careful to recognize that each portion of our lives should be lived out in faithfulness to our purpose. We are here to send the Gospel to the four corners and bring glory to God, for "in him we live and move and have our being."

> *God that made the world and all things therein, seeing that he is Lord of heaven and earth, dwelleth not in temples made with hands; Neither is worshipped with men's hands, as though he needed any thing, seeing he giveth to all life, and breath, and all things; And hath made of one blood all nations of men for to dwell on all the face of the earth, and hath determined the times before appointed, and the bounds of their habitation; That they should seek the Lord, if haply they might feel after him, and find him, though he be not far from every one of us: For in him we live, and move, and have our being; as certain also of your own poets have said, For we are also his offspring. Acts 17:24–28*

But sometimes we can get these things right but miss an even bigger opportunity that our hearts and homes can invest in—the missional opportunity of a home overflowing with the love of Christ.

Now don't get me wrong. I know how busy we all are. I often call myself a multi-passionate creative, but let's face it, I'm just crazy busy with all the things. I'm a wife, mom, author, speaker, musician, teacher, entrepreneur, homeschooler—should I keep going? But having a lot on my plate doesn't cancel out the Great Commission. All these things are well and good and can actually help me continue to fulfill my purpose, but I am often guilty of governing my day by checklists and missing the opportunities to love people that God brings to me.

I have the tendency to take on too many things—even good things—and then become stressed out, unreasonable, and downright cranky. There's a whole incident I call "Muffins for Jesus" . . .

Hospitality in Scripture

And the LORD appeared unto him in the plains of Mamre: and he sat in the tent door in the heat of the day; And he lift up his eyes and looked, and, lo, three men stood by him: and when he saw them, he ran to meet them from the tent door, and bowed himself toward the ground, And said, My Lord, if now I have found favour in thy sight, pass not away, I pray thee, from thy servant: Let a little water, I pray you, be fetched, and wash your feet, and rest yourselves under the tree: And I will fetch a morsel of bread, and comfort ye your hearts; after that ye shall pass on: for therefore are ye come to your servant. And they said, So do, as thou hast said. Genesis 18:1–5

I had the idea to bake fresh muffins and deliver them to visiting families the week after they came to our church. Everyone loved this idea and added to it! We even picked special boxes to serve them in and put stickers on the packages with the church name and logo. Who wouldn't want a box of muffins? My problem is that many times I have these ideas, but then I feel it's my job to execute them. That's right, I'm terrible at delegating. The worst!

Hindsight being 20/20, I should have asked someone to volunteer to bake the muffins, or box the muffins, or buy the boxes or even print the labels. But I didn't, and you can likely guess how Mondays went down at my house when my kids were little! Instead of having many hands support the work, it was just my own hands, and it seemed like every Monday the printer was jammed. Or one of the kids would be sick and I had to figure out how to get more boxes because we had more visitors than I had anticipated. There were so many muffins, and never once did I ask if someone else *wanted* to do it. In no time at all, I was grumpy, ill-tempered, and frustrated. No one knew how much I dreaded Mondays and those muffins. Eventually, I was so overwhelmed that I had to admit I needed help. I had been operating in my own strength and my flesh became weak.

When we resent the work, our hearts are downright wrong. This reminds me of the very clear picture in James of bitter and sweet water not flowing from the same place.

Out of the same mouth come blessing and cursing. My brothers, this should not be! Can both fresh water and bitter water flow from the same spring? James 3:10–11

Our homes are an extension of our faith, and if we are not willing to open them at any time, for anyone who has need, we might be forgetting that these temporary things that God has given us to enjoy are in all reality His alone.

Every good and perfect gift is from above . . . James 1:17

A proper view of His ownership helps me keep my perspective on the reality that my home should be missional.

I asked friends on Facebook recently to tell me what they think of when they hear the word "hospitality." Here are some of the responses:

- Fellowship with church people
- Discipleship
- Witnessing
- Open home, any time, for any reason
- Friendship
- Food
- Meeting needs, whether that means food, shelter, or friendship
- Focusing hospitality on those who cannot reciprocate
- Inviting others into our ordinary everyday lives
- Being willing to invite others in even if our home isn't "ready"
- The early church led us by example in this exercise of practicing hospitality.

But what does that look like in real life? I may not ever feel like my home is "perfect" enough, but there are a few simple things that help me feel prepared for drop-in guests:

Our homes are an extension of our faith, and if we are not willing to open them, we might be forgetting that these temporary things that God has given us to enjoy are in all reality His alone.

- Certain areas in the home need to be fairly neat and orderly, or "pick-up-able" in five minutes or fewer. This requires a decluttering and some furniture or accessories that store things out of sight while still being lovely in the room.
- A supply of lemonade mix and special cookies.
- Coffee and/or tea, and crackers and cheese or fruit.

Why? Because a missional mindset plans ahead to make someone feel special. While yet nameless, we want that person who comes into our space to feel welcomed and wanted.

But please don't hear me say, don't invite people in if the laundry is strewn across the living room waiting to be folded, or mail piled up on the table, or you are flat out of drinks and snacks. No, not at all. As a matter of fact, invite people into the mess and let them see reality. Call and order a pizza if necessary, but by all means bring them on in and have a good laugh about reality. I've been there, and honestly, these have been some of the greatest moments for me. As much as I cringe to have others see my humanity, these moments rip off my facade of having it all together and allow me to connect in real ways with others struggling to get through life *and the laundry* together.

More than anything, our homes will be missional in nature to our families, friends, neighbors, and strangers if our hearts are overflowing with the love of Christ. A heart spilling over with Him will inevitably be appealing to those we come in contact with and, as they observe us, we can invite them into the realities of our lives and walk this journey together. And by His grace, perhaps we will have the opportunity to share the truth of the Gospel and enjoy an eternity in Heaven together because we kept our hearts open and our homes available!

Friends, don't overcomplicate this. I believe that if we let the lack of things or space or time hinder us from being hospitable, it's our error. And frankly, our disobedience.

Living life together means discipleship, walking side by side, experiencing the highs and lows of daily living. This could include those who need a longer stay than a meal, or just one night. It might mean bringing in those who have a need from another country—perhaps a foreign exchange student, asylum seeker, or refugee.

A missional mindset plans ahead to make someone feel special.

Hospitality encompasses both long-term stays—perhaps the homeless, jobless, or a mom and babe in need—as well as "short-term" meals, coffee and cookies, or a late night chat over cups of steaming tea. We may also have the opportunity to help those who need shelter during a disaster, whether personal (bankruptcy, marriage crisis) or natural (tornado, hurricane, flood, etc.). Sometimes hospitality means delivering a meal, running an errand, or cleaning someone else's home.

Hospitality can be a challenge for introverts. Having to be "on" as a hostess can create tension and stress in certain personalities more than others. But the Bible doesn't give us a pass because something is difficult. Perhaps this is a way to carry your cross and follow Him more closely. I always view this as an opportunity for my weakness to reveal His strength. His glory in my story.

Biblical hospitality is letting people into your actual life, not your ideal life.

It's a heart for serving others. This can only come from a heart that is led by the Holy Spirit, demonstrating the fruit of the spirit.

Biblical hospitality is loving well on purpose and being intentional.

It is claiming and dedicating my home to honor Christ.

It requires being willing to have difficult, strange, or challenging conversations and discussions with others. It might include being challenged in our beliefs.

Hospitality is a reminder to bless, not impress.

It requires being a good listener.

True hospitality is loving people who are unlikely to repay us.

Biblical hospitality is more than inviting someone to a meal, it's inviting someone into your life.

Being filled up with Christ means being poured out.

Let this mind be in you, which was also in Christ Jesus: Who, being in the form of God, thought it not robbery to be equal with God: But made himself of no reputation, and took upon him the form of a servant, and was made in the likeness of men. Philippians 2:5–7

When we desire to live our lives like Jesus did, we must learn to follow His example. He reminded his disciples that he came not to be served, but to serve. And not just serve, but to also give his life as a ransom for many.

Even as the Son of man came not to be ministered unto, but to minister, and to give his life a ransom for many. Matthew 20:28

This vision and expectation should also be ours. We should desire to serve, to be served, and to give our all with the expectation of nothing in return. This is our vision of hospitality—sacrificial

service to our families, friends, neighbors, church, community, travelers, and strangers—all with Jesus and for Jesus.

Read through Romans 12. Verse 1 reminds us that we are a "living sacrifice" and verse 10 is the reminder that we are to "prefer others," while verse 13 reminds us that as believers we should be "given to hospitality."

Moving the Roadblocks

What keeps us from embracing hospitality as God intends? Here are some things my Facebook tribe mentioned:

- Busyness
- Packed calendar (church activities, children's activities, work, and school)
- Lack of money
- Lack of nice things
- Fear of judgment
- Lack of obedience
- Lack of desire
- Selfishness
- It requires sacrifice
- It requires planning, especially for families with small children
- Concern that guests will be allergic to pets
- Pride
- It's uncomfortable and invades our privacy
- Perfectionism
- It's too easy to offend someone who is different from us culturally or politically
- Rejection hurts
- Fear of failure and disappointment

Perhaps one of these reasons resonates with you, or maybe you have other reasons for not being more obedient to the call of Biblical hospitality. Let's try to eliminate the things that hinder us from being more hospitable in all of our relationships with others.

Extraordinary Hospitality for Ordinary Christians

It may help to remember that we are called to hospitality, but not necessarily to entertaining. This should eliminate the enormous burden so many of us place on ourselves to have the best, supply the best, and take everyone everywhere, which is entertaining.

We also need to be mindful that how we practice hospitality will encourage or discourage others to practice hospitality themselves. I try to remind myself of this very fact when I'm running around the house preparing for company and commanding that everyone help. No one enjoys company if Momma is a crazy person trying to prepare. None of my children will want to invite others into their homes one day if they see how much "trouble" it was for Mom while they were growing up. I have to be so mindful of my reactions and actions in these moments because I truly want each of them to benefit and practice hospitality in their own homes.

Other Biblical Examples

Fellowship, care, and support are often displayed in the Bible through a shared meal. We see Jesus demonstrating this not only in the first miracle He performed at the wedding in Cana by turning water into wine, but also in the upper room as the crucifixion was drawing near. His example and others' model for us true Biblical hospitality being not only the fellowship of believers but also nonbelievers with a desire for sharing the love of Christ together. The key here is that we should always place an emphasis on Christ whenever we invite others in; otherwise it just becomes entertaining.

At the end of the day, it's really about our hearts. Whether we are serving an elaborate meal on fine china and a beautifully set table or we are just pouring a quick cup of coffee, it's always the heart that counts.

When my heart is out of alignment and is focused on myself, then I will believe that hospitality has a long list of requirements. When my heart is focused on God, hospitality flows easily from a spirit of gentleness, goodness, and kindness no matter the food served, the linens used, or the space available.

Practicing hospitality regularly doesn't mean I'm always fixing food, preparing bedrooms for overnight guests, or even doing all the work. I might be allowing others to use my space for their gatherings. Or it might be that I need to allow others to help out when they offer. This can be tricky, especially for those of us who struggle with letting people know we have a need. Learning to receive help is an important part of the process of hospitality. If we don't let others know what they could do, or we are too proud to allow them to help, we rob them of a blessing.

The examples of the power of hospitality in Scripture continue on: Naomi and Ruth were hungry widows who received food and kindness from Boaz and thus became partakers in Christ's story. Zarephath received miraculous provision because Elisha arrived at her home in I Kings 17. Jesus supplied large crowds with fish and bread, feeding their hungry bodies as he fed their souls with truth. And, most important, Jesus gathers people to Himself, proving again that God opens doors and invites all of us in.

Tracing these stories through Scripture should awaken a desire in us to duplicate God's kind of table. We should feel excited to live life together, which will always include meals, community, and fellowship and will eliminate boundaries and restrictions on who is allowed or wanted. Our gatherings can include believers and unbelievers, creating community where each individual can feel seen, known, and loved.

It is worth noting that the New Testament teaches that our church leaders should be known for their hospitality. While that will look different among the variety of leaders in a variety of churches, if you have a desire to lead, especially in a church setting, you should be recognized as being hospitable.

A bishop then must be blameless, the husband of one wife, vigilant, sober, of good behaviour, given to hospitality, apt to teach . . . 1 Timothy 3:2

For a bishop must be blameless, as the steward of God; not selfwilled, not soon angry, not given to wine, no striker, not given to filthy lucre; But a lover of hospitality, a lover of good men, sober, just, holy, temperate . . . Titus 1:7–8

Hospitality is an act of righteous, godly behavior. When the angels journeyed to Sodom and Gomorrah in search of a righteous man, only Lot and his family were set apart to be saved. Lot was deemed righteous because of his hospitality.

And he pressed upon them greatly; and they turned in unto him, and entered into his house; and he made them a feast, and did bake unleavened bread, and they did eat. Genesis 19:3

Sodom and Gomorrah were judged for a variety of sins, including their lack of hospitality.

As I live, saith the Lord GOD, Sodom thy sister hath not done, she nor her daughters, as thou hast done, thou and thy daughters. Behold, this was the iniquity of thy sister Sodom, pride, fulness of bread, and abundance of idleness was in her and in her daughters, neither did she strengthen the hand of the poor and needy. And they were haughty, and committed abomination before me: therefore I took them away as I saw good. Ezekiel 16:48–50

Hebrews reminds us that our guests may be more than they appear.

Be not forgetful to entertain strangers: for thereby some have entertained angels unawares. Hebrews 13:2

When we offer a helping hand, an open door, or a meal to a stranger, we might actually be assisting a ministering angel or messenger from the Lord. If we are in the habit of offering to help anyone in need, anytime they need it, we could very likely have a Hebrews 13 encounter. Abraham and Sarah, Lot, Gideon, and Manoah all entertained strangers who were actually special messengers from God.

Because generosity should be the mark of a Christian, we learn from Luke that the measure with which we are generous is the same measure that will be returned.

Give, and it shall be given unto you; good measure, pressed down, and shaken together, and running over, shall men give into your bosom. For with the same measure that ye mete withal it shall be measured to you again. Luke 6:38

This should never be our motivation for how we live, of course, but it does help us to remember that we can never ever outgive God.

Entertainment vs. Hospitality

"We may go so far as to invite someone over for dinner, but we tend to do so with those who look like us, talk like us, believe like us, and act like us. And before we even consider having these friends around, we'll carefully engineer our homes and shape and polish our personas to communicate the best version of who we are—or at least the image that we hope to project."[1]

Often, the kind of hospitality we try to practice is different than what the Bible encourages. Because of our pride, we want to project a certain image of our homes and our lives, so we embark on hours of cleaning, rack up massive grocery bills, and even purchase new home decor, furniture, and linens. Now, it's possible God is calling you to do those things and spend that money to bless others, in which case, do it! But more likely, it is our desire to impress others with our style, our financial stability, or our generosity. Here, the focus remains firmly on ourselves and all we are doing. Even if we don't realize we are doing  that, our human natures constantly pressure us to do more, be more, and have more rather than focusing on God and His provision and goodness. Pinterest and Instagram can offer us inspiration, but too often they instead push us into some fake ideal that is the opposite of the intimacy and personal relationships we are seeking when we long to connect in true hospitality.

Once again, we have bought into the lie that what we are, what we have, and what we do could ever be enough, rather than depending fully on God's grace and the truth of the gospel. We cannot sustain a life in which we're continually overextending ourselves. We will eventually break down and push others away. Again, this is the opposite of living life together.

I recently shared with a women's group that one of the deepest needs we all feel as humans is to be seen. We long to be seen in a world that constantly overlooks us. Whether we are average or exceptional, large or small, wealthy or poor, we long to be seen because then we can be known. Being known is so risky though, isn't it? Being vulnerable with people creates the very real possibility that we will be rejected. And rejection is devastating. We long to be loved no matter what—and that's just how Jesus loves us. Because of Jesus's love for me, I can love my neighbor by seeing, knowing, and still loving, unconditionally.

The longer I'm alive, the more I'm convinced this process must be learned. At my core, I'm selfish and self-serving. I look to my own needs and have to train myself instead to look for and at others. Looking people in the eye is one of the things we have to teach our children, isn't it? It doesn't always come naturally, and we have to work at teaching them to really look and see people. It's the same way for us as adults. We get busy, wrapped up in our own stuff, whether it's work or stress or goals, and we forget to slow down and really see others. When we see people as Jesus sees them, we learn that first and foremost He wants us to love Him with all our hearts, and then love others. These are the great commandments. I can't love if I don't see. And I can't truly, deeply love with understanding if I don't take time to get to know people.

When I'm running in typical Martha fashion, I don't really talk with my guests. I have to intentionally make myself sit down in those times. It doesn't make the work go away or lessen the load I feel to provide for my guests, but it physically reminds me to keep my focus on the people in my presence, versus the checklist on my counter. True hospitality and friendship encourage me to listen—to listen to others in what they are saying and are not saying. Sometimes people need the space of quiet in order to express their feelings, knowing that they are in a safe environment in a place where they can unload their troubles and fears. This is when I learn to be quiet and still. I learn to listen to what the need may really be and how I can best meet that need.

I can't truly, deeply love with understanding if I don't take time to get to know people.

> We don't all have stages from which to speak, but we all have homes with doors that can be opened.

We may not have an immediate solution for someone in need. Rather, many times I just learn how to pray more specifically for someone. Being ready to go to the Lord in prayer for my friend, neighbor, or random stranger and pray with specificity means that I took time to really hear their heart and the core of their need. Sometimes really listening requires that I initiate the conversation by sharing my own struggle. Again, this requires vulnerability that is uncomfortable. Or it requires that I learn how to create conversation by asking questions and pursuing respectful discussion, even if I disagree with something being said.

We have to learn to listen with an ear to understanding the heart of what's being said versus waiting for our turn to talk or defend our beliefs. This doesn't mean we will always agree with everyone, or that we have to set aside our convictions. Rather, it means that we respectfully learn to communicate that while we don't agree with everything that person is saying, we will still listen and work to understand another perspective. This fosters an environment of openness and opportunity. You never know when someone will want to know more about the God you say you love because you gave them the opportunity to explain why they don't believe He exists. Being respectful goes a long way to being heard.

When I think of using my home, truly leveraging my home for the kingdom, it becomes all about trying to get the message of the Gospel to as many people as possible. I am able to reach people that others might not be able to because of where God has placed me geographically, or in the job he has provided, or in the church he has us serving. We each have a different audience of people who God wants us to reach. We don't all have stages from which to speak, but we all have homes with doors that can be opened.

Hospitality in Scripture

And Jacob sod pottage: and Esau came from the field, and he was faint: And Esau said to Jacob, Feed me, I pray thee, with that same red pottage; for I am faint: therefore was his name called Edom. And Jacob said, Sell me this day thy birthright. And Esau said, Behold, I am at the point to die: and what profit shall this birthright do to me? And Jacob said, Swear to me this day; and he sware unto him: and he sold his birthright unto Jacob. Then Jacob gave Esau bread and pottage of lentiles; and he did eat and drink, and rose up, and went his way: thus Esau despised his birthright. Genesis 25:29–34

A Right Attitude

And above all things have fervent charity among yourselves: for charity shall cover the multitude of sins. Use hospitality one to another without grudging. As every man hath received the gift, even so minister the same one to another, as good stewards of the manifold grace of God. 1 Peter 4:8–10

These verses build on the instruction to practice hospitality and reminds us that at the end of the day, our attitude is of utmost importance—we are to practice hospitality without complaining.

We learn from the Old Testament that we have been blessed to be a blessing. We see the example over and over, but it is especially clear in Genesis 12:2 when God says to Abraham, "I will bless you and make your name great, so that you will be a blessing." In addition, we understand that the phrasing from the New Testament in Acts teaches us that it is more blessed to give than receive.

Yea, ye yourselves know, that these hands have ministered unto my necessities, and to them that were with me. I have shewed you all things, how that so labouring ye ought to support the weak, and to remember the words of the Lord Jesus, how he said, It is more blessed to give than to receive. Acts 20:34–35

We can approach hospitality with *joy*, understanding that we receive a blessing in the midst of working to serve others. And if we don't feel particularly joyful, or don't naturally have a gift for hospitality, we should pray that God would fill us with the emotions to back up our actions. Sometimes we serve because we are supposed to, but I believe God will bless by providing the emotions to encourage and fulfill us as well. Always be prayerful about hospitality.

At the core of our service to others, Biblical hospitality includes love, and because we have been so loved by Christ, we can overflow in love to others.

Pray that God would fill us with the emotions to back up our actions.

Taste and See

Taste and see that the Lord is good. Psalm 34:8

I've always enjoyed the word picture this creates. Good food just can't be beat. Living just south of Memphis, it's all about BBQ. There's nothing like it, and just thinking about baby back ribs or pulled pork creates such a desire to eat it that I can almost taste it even now. When we taste and see that the Lord is good, we are actively in pursuit of a relationship with Him. We are longing to be in His presence, and just the very thought of His goodness should make us desire to be with Him more. We want to be in close proximity to Him, and we learn as we dwell with Him just how good He is.

We see the evidence of His goodness by the way he cares for our needs and so much more. Many times He provides extra—the wants, the desires, the seemingly small things. But He never blesses us to just sit with it and be blessed. Rather, He wants us to take the blessing and overflow onto others around us. We just can't do that if we don't actively seek out ways to interact and connect and talk with each other.

And I get it.

It's not convenient. It's hard, and many times it is messy. Connecting with others who don't think like us, talk like us, or look like us can get especially complicated. But how enriching it is in our lives to reach out beyond our normal sphere of influence and really connect.

Having raised three children, my husband and I know just how overwhelming juggling schedules can be. We have active schedules even now, but certain seasons could easily see us running around from afternoon through the evening every night of the week. Having a meal together around a table was rare. We had to work to put family dinner on the calendar, and sometimes it still didn't work out. We limited the activities to one per kid, but that's still three activities a week!

If you are reading and feeling that there's no way to do any of the things I've mentioned, I understand. There are certain seasons where this is more challenging than others. Take advantage of the days your immediate family has together and make everyone gather. As you make it a habit to gather, then it will be easier to invite others to join you. Invite them into your crazy chaos and see what happens.

One thing we learned through the years is that sometimes people actually enjoy that chaos. I have always tried to mask the crazy or at least try to put the lipstick on the pig, but sometimes you can't, and that's when our authenticity and transparency pay off. When we reveal our reality and our true selves, people instantly take down their guard and connect. When our kids were small, we hosted a singles Bible study in our home. We had a mix of some church youth group kids that had grown out of youth group but hadn't left home and military guys who would roll through for training and needed a place to belong. Tuesday nights we'd invite them all into our space for dinner and Bible study and that's when everything always fell apart. I mean it—if it could go wrong, it did. One time, the baby was in the Pack 'n Play while I was cleaning house and somehow she got the childproof lid off Advil bottle and consumed . . . who knows how many? They were everywhere—in the Pack 'n Play, outside on the floor, and possibly inside her. So off to the emergency room we went. (Thankfully, she was fine.)

Bedtimes were always fun, too. The girls never wanted to go to sleep while there was a house full of people. The FOMO was so real—they didn't want to miss anything. There would be child arguments, sibling rivalry, tooth pulling. . . . I was sure our home was more chaotic than anyone else's.

I often felt so defeated during those years. We were often a hot mess of toddler meltdowns, emergency room visits, and burnt bread. Amid the fellowship and meals we shared together, I was often flustered and frustrated, wondering if anything was making a difference for the kingdom when my family was such a distraction.

But God, in His grace, used that time in my life and in the lives of those singles. And before you think I deserve any credit here, I don't. I was often out of sorts, and while outwardly willing to host, I was inwardly unwilling to be useful because, to be honest, I was tired and trying to do it all during those years.

If I knew then what I know now, I would have relaxed a good bit and realized the kids were being kids. They were being real-life examples of family, and we were including others in our mess. The military kids felt like they were home, and that's just what they needed. We loaded them up with food and some truths of God's word and I pray the impact lasts to this day.

What I mostly want you to know from this story is that I wasn't someone special or super woman or super spiritual. I was just being willing to put to use what God had blessed us with, and you can, too.

Disasters and Opportunities

There's nothing like a disaster to bring folks together. When we recognize that we have more than the person next to us and we have the opportunity to act and meet a need, we are driven to action.

> *Withhold not good from them to whom it is due, when it is in the power of thine hand to do it.*
> *Proverbs 3:27*

This is so fresh on my mind right now because we literally just had two different tornadoes touch down in our community the same evening. Just fifteen miles away from our home, the devastation is extensive. There are people without power, water, safe shelter, or food.

But the outpouring of help has been beautiful to watch. Local Facebook groups organized volunteers with one person making a cobbler, one restaurant donating meals for 400–500 people, and dozens of additional people delivering food to those who couldn't get out. Others grabbed chainsaws and showed up where they could help the most. Others with means are donating money to pay for hotel rooms for people to be able to stay in while they figure life out. People are donating space to gather and create a command center of sorts to bring in donations, to gather and share information, or for respite from the work. Calls went out for donations, and, within a short amount of time, they had to start turning them away.

It's been beautiful to watch. Especially during a disaster, we are not worrying about giving out of our abundance; rather we are compelled to open doors to say, what's mine is yours. People aren't thinking about whether or not they'll ever get repaid.

The work will go on for some time, but the reality is that as we return to our daily lives, work and school and the rest, time will cause many to forget. A month from now, some will still be trying to get on their feet, but the meals will probably not be delivered or even offered, and the donations will dry up. It's the cycle, unfortunately, that in urgent situations many of us deliver, but in the day-to-day living, and when a trial or situation goes on for a long period, we tire of the drain on our time, belongings, and emotions.

When people are in crisis, they need just a few important things—safety and shelter, sustenance, and someone who cares. Making a difference in these circumstances doesn't require fancy. It requires willingness and an open door.

When people are in crisis, they need just a few important things—safety and shelter, sustenance, and someone who cares.

Loving My Neighbor

In some ways, loving your neighbors in the midst of busy everyday life may feel harder than during a crisis. Without the adrenaline and urgency of a disaster, we can become complacent, too wrapped up in our own needs and problems to notice anyone else's.

If someone asks us, "Do you love your neighbor?" our answer would immediately be "yes!" I don't know anyone that wouldn't say that they love their neighbor. But in the nitty-gritty of life, do we really love our neighbor?

Do we love them enough to have a conversation with them?

Do we love them enough to care about their lives?

Are we too selfish, too busy, too overwhelmed with our own problems to try to shoulder or carry the burdens of someone else?

And are my neighbors only the folks who live on either side of me, or is it the person I come into contact with at the grocery store or the gas station?

Do I love them enough to carry on a conversation once every six months, or enough to invite them into my home to live with me?

Do I love them enough to pick them up after their car breaks down, or drive them to a chemo appointment, or to literally sit and cry and pray together?

Do I love my neighbor enough to preach the truth of the Gospel to them with not just my words but also with the way I live my life?

How do I cross the barriers that divide us—Democrat or Replublication, pro- or anti-gun rights, pro- or anti-vaccine choice, public or private school, black or white, flat earth or round?

I wish there was a guide for every circumstance that would tell me do this, say this, don't do that, and absolutely never say that. Because that would be so much easier for the rule-following, type A, overachieving me. I want someone to have figured out the exact formula, and I will simply duplicate it. I will do the hard work, but I don't want to make mistakes. And what I fear most of all is that there is a mess to be made when I am in the trenches of seeking to fulfill God's command of loving my neighbor. I'm afraid truly connecting with others who are unlike me may wreak havoc with what I believe to be true and hold on to as reality in my own life.

The tears roll down my face as I type today, because I feel it deep in my soul. This understanding of loving as Jesus loves and of caring for people at their very core, especially the unlovely, will require mess. And I hate mess. I come apart at the seams with mess, ugliness, difficulty, challenge, and conflict. But sometimes those are the circumstances in which Jesus does His most amazing work.

And it's not just the people who come knocking on our door who we are called to serve. We are meant to seek out people to help. Jesus had many people that came to him because they heard of his miracles and they wanted to know Him. But he didn't set up shop in one corner of Galilee and hang out a shingle with office hours. He was always on the go into a new city, by walking, by boat, by being on the move going *to* people in need. Some people didn't even know they had a need, but He knew it.

How many people do I miss connecting with because I am only limiting myself to the people who call my name, who touch my shoulder or send a text?

Let me say I don't necessarily think that we are all selfish, or that we are defiant or disobedient to God's call to hospitality. I think we just lose our focus in the midst of all the shiny things. The distractions. Raising a family, working our jobs, even doing ministry can bog us down, and we forget to stay focused on the true prize of living our purpose. When we keep the main thing the main thing, we can truly love God and love others.

If you struggle as I do with being selfish, begin following God's command to die to self, daily. Begin the process of loosening your grip on your time, your possessions, and your rights and learn to let go. In this process and step of obedience, I believe we can find the earnestness that is required in seeking out that neighbor who needs you.

Decluttering

Clutter is the physical manifestation of unmade decisions fueled by procrastination.[2]

—Christina Scalise

One of the things I've observed in my own married life through the years is the fact that my stuff can keep me from people. And at the end of the day, that makes me sad. Possessions shouldn't keep us from people. Whether the problem is too many or too few, it doesn't really matter. Time and again, we allow things to interfere with our relationships.

When I can't have guests over on the spur of the moment because the house is a mess, I'm allowing my stuff to interfere.

When I have to clean for hours on end to prepare for company and I gripe or get cranky with my family because they are not doing enough to help, then I'm allowing my stuff to control my relationships.

I propose that we should work to live in a better way. Not only because it will bring peace and happiness to my people inside my home, but also because it will bring a sense of control. While I know and understand I am never fully in control of all the things, knowing that I can "right the ship" in quick order will give me confidence to extend the invitation to that young couple who could use some encouragement, the family that we just haven't had a chance to get to know, or the stranger who needs a hand.

A better way must mean living with intention versus flying by the seat of my pants. Living with intention requires planning.

My friend Kathy came to our home once—just dropped in. I was horrified. No makeup on, in the standard sweatpants-and-sweatshirt uniform of my early motherhood and clean laundry strewn from one end of the living room to the other. I was overwhelmed with shame. Shame that I had no time to hide the laundry (I had a glass front door, after all), no choice but to answer the door and face the music.

That day I learned such a valuable lesson. It's been twenty years and I can still remember my embarrassment at my mess, and her gracious response. I remember being more relaxed with her sitting with me in my mess than many other times where the perfect cleanup had occurred just minutes or hours before. She didn't even seem to be bothered by my mess. Rather, she sat in the middle of it helping me fold burp cloths, baby dresses, and God only knows what else. We talked and worked side by side in true relationship, because real friends don't have to hide from each other. Being authentic means being vulnerable—no masks, no hiding. Kathy taught me the value of opening the door and releasing the fake burden of hiding my clutter, clean though it was. She taught me the value of having a friend sit down and work with me in the middle of my mess—not isolated and alone. She shared later that I had encouraged her by allowing her in even though I had laundry everywhere. She had no idea I was so embarrassed and mortified. Instead, she was encouraged to live her life in the same way.

It's a lesson not soon forgotten. On the days I wish to hide and pretend I can't be with anyone because my mess is too great, I am reminded of this lesson with Kathy.

Isn't this often how we approach our relationship with God? We try to hide from Him. We make a mess and leave behind the clutter of sinfulness until He knocks on the door. But He's that friend that ignores the mess and sits and works with us. Because the reality is, He's already done the work and, in His eyes, we are made clean. Washed in the blood and reconciled to Him means no more work on my end—He's done it all. When I hide, it's guilt and shame from the enemy working to create a divide and division in my relationship.

Why Is Clutter a Problem?

Clutter becomes a problem because it takes away negative space. Negative space is actually a positive idea! When we address the concept of negative space in design, we are talking about more white space on our walls, shelves, and in our rooms. White or neutral space creates a sense of calm and order. Conversely, when there's too little negative space, a room can make one feel anxious, scattered, and uncomfortable.

Accumulating more stuff will never satisfy those empty spots in our soul.

Clutter also inhabits our hearts and minds, making us less useful for the kingdom and more like the rest of the world around us. We become cluttered in our hearts when we hold on to unconfessed sin, incorrect priorities, and fear and anxiety instead of relying on God. We become attached to our stuff, instead of relying on God to supply all our needs and fill us up, and it ends up choking out our desire for Him and our pursuit of holiness. Accumulating more stuff will never satisfy those empty spots in our soul.

Learning to take regular assessments of our negative space, both physically and spiritually, will help us keep both our homes and hearts open to pursue Christ with freedom and a holy passion. Hearts aflame for His purpose can ignite our homes into discipling environments where his truth can abound and work freely.

Less Is More

Let us also lay aside every encumbrance, and the sin which so easily entangles us and let us run with endurance the race that is set before us. Hebrews 12:1b

Have you ever felt overwhelmed in your own home? I mean, where you feel desperate to get away from the excess stuff that you can't seem to manage or organize anymore? I think, my friend, that means that you have too much stuff. Excess stuff weighs us down with the burden of finding places to keep and organize it all. From pillows to lamps, to collectibles and dishes, stuff crowds our homes and our lives.

The best course of action is to eliminate the clutter; don't just organize it. Because organized clutter is still clutter. Whether it exists out in the open or in the secret places, it is still excess. Let's not even discuss the financial burden it brings! How much does it cost us to have too much stuff? When it begins to overflow the closets, the attic, and the garage, we rent storage units to keep it all in. This financial burden can be oppressive, and it exists because we just can't seem to let things go.

> Eliminating those things that crowd my heart and creating space for what Christ desires me to have instead helps me become more like Him.

I recently posted about releasing clutter and excess on Instagram and got some pushback on this idea, as if it wasn't realistic. Why is that? Why do we have this endless pursuit of acquiring more; is it the American Dream? Or is it just plain greed, or perhaps a sense that we never have "enough?" Perhaps you are a parent and want to provide for your kids all those things that you didn't have growing up. I'd caution you to be ever so vigilant to keep that in check. Far too many times, that desire to provide beyond basic needs creates a danger zone of clutter and chaos. *Chasing stuff never satisfies.* Chaos and mayhem reign with excess and our souls get cramped until we can't breathe.

Isn't that just like sin? We all deal with sin. All of us. Whether it is a recurring sin we struggle to get the victory over or new roots of sin in our hearts, no one is exempt. This consumerism isn't just rampant and evident in our homes. It's choking our hearts as well. Our hearts are buried in layers of sin, unresolved conflicts with others, anxiety, and care. Keeping a short account of our sins with the Lord is vital to our Christian walk and growth. Eliminating those things that crowd my heart and creating space for what Christ desires me to have instead helps me become more like Him. Ridding our homes of clutter and creating a simple style helps us enjoy our space more. The same holds true in our hearts. Following Christ is only possible when we purge sin and pursue holiness.

Clear It Out

Let us draw near with a sincere heart in full assurance of faith, having our hearts sprinkled clean from an evil conscience and our bodies washed with pure water. Hebrews 10:21–23

When you are first setting a room or moving into a home, all the little accessories and pieces are lined up in a hallway or garage and they eventually find their spots. And at some point, they've been there so long you don't even see them anymore, and then you buy more stuff and the original stuff just gets buried.

A complete purge is probably necessary. Maybe not a full-fledged "KonMari" to decide if things still bring you joy, but a complete removal of the things out of a room or closet, so that they can be brought out in the light, sorted, and tossed or set back in an appropriate spot, or given to someone else who has a need. Many times we can sell the items we have in a garage sale, on eBay or Facebook Marketplace, or to a consignment store and make a little money that we could put back into our household budget. I don't know anyone who wouldn't like to have a little more margin in the bank account!

Here's the thing, though: Sin is the same way in our hearts. When we are not paying attention, it accumulates. If we are not daily confessing and forsaking, we are only compounding the problem of sin in our hearts. This stifles our relationship with God!

Create in me a clean heart, O God, and renew a right spirit within me. Psalm 51:10

Praise the Lord! He is faithful and promises to restore us when we approach sin in this manner. Let's be diligent to root out and weed out the clutter of sin from our hearts.

How Much Is Enough?

How many T-shirts can you wear at one time? In one week? In two weeks? How many pairs of shoes can you really wear?

What would life look like if, before purchasing something, we stopped and thought, *is this really something I need?* For many items, if we were to wait a week or a month before hitting that "buy" button, we'd realize we don't actually even want the thing anymore!

Many of us are especially prone to over-accumulating things for our kids. How many toys can they really play with? What if, instead, for holidays and birthday we bought a family membership to the zoo, the amusement park, or saved up for a family vacation? Wouldn't experiences and family time matter more than that fifty-piece playset that in three months will be broken and discarded?

What if you could bless someone else with that excess instead of piling up more stuff in your own home?

It reminds me of the story in Matthew 19 of the rich young ruler. He followed all the rules, he obeyed the law, and had much wealth. Jesus told him to sell it all and follow Him, and the ruler walked away sad because he didn't want to let go of his possessions.

His stuff kept him from Jesus.

Or the passage in Luke 12 that talks about a man who had very fertile land and abundant crops. He kept running out of room to store all the harvest, so he built more warehouses to store it. But Jesus reminded the people that when he died, he couldn't take it with him. What good would all that abundance do him in the afterlife?

I truly believe the lesson here is not that abundance is wrong, but rather that abundance is meant to be turned into a blessing for someone else. Instead of buying things just to accumulate more and more stuff, we should instead be working hard to be able to care for others who have a need.

The problem is that instead of allowing God's blessings to flow through us to others, we block that flow by hanging on to everything for ourselves. The same way water stagnates and becomes unsanitary, we become putrid, unuseful, and disgusting when we accumulate just to satisfy our own lustful and selfish desires.

When we actively make an effort to provide for others and give to His kingdom, He is the one who says His blessings will overflow out of the storehouse, and that you can build more and still can't contain it. He will continue to bless over and over and over again.

The parable of the talents (Matthew 25:15–29) applies here as well. We learn that God gives us certain resources to not just be comfortable or to stay the same but with the purpose of growing, changing, and using the things He give us. I believe this isn't just in relation to money, but also our homes, our food, our belongings and time. Every single thing that He blesses us with is meant to be used for a bigger purpose: bringing Him glory and blessing others.

The talents also teach us that when we do the opposite and bury rather than develop or give away or use the gifts He's given, we will eventually lose those things God has blessed us with.

When we have been given a home to live in, I truly believe we are to work to maintain it, make it the best that it can be, and work hard to keep it orderly and decent.

A Decluttered Mind

Finally, brethren, whatsoever things are true, whatsoever things are honest, whatsoever things are just, whatsoever things are pure, whatsoever things are lovely, whatsoever things are of good report . . . think on these things. Philippians 4:8

I was reminded recently about the power of what we are consistently allowing into our minds. Whether we are listening to music or talk radio, news broadcasts or movies, or reading books and newspapers, our minds are inundated with messages that people with an agenda want us to hear. And if we hear it often enough, it will fully saturate our minds and assimilate into our patterns of thinking. And honestly, the devil would love nothing more than to saturate our minds with his filth.

The reality is that if the devil can keep us distracted by chasing pleasure, annoyed by opposing views of our friends and neighbors, and numbed to the reality of sinful viewpoints and attitudes, he can keep us from being an effective witness for Christ. Reality TV, junk music, and movies that don't actually support or encourage our worldview are continually cluttering our minds with conflicting messages.

If, rather, we filter each and every thing that we allow in our homes through this verse, how much do you think our hearts and homes might change? I would like to propose, as well, that I don't think it's enough for us to remove the clutter and create the negative space, but we must also be careful what we consume in the future so that we can be ready for what God wants us to do. Bible study, prayer, meditation, and Scripture memory all take time. And time is one of those things that we all complain we don't have enough of. How much more time could we carve out though, if we eliminated just one show? What about eliminating just one news broadcast or one movie, and instead used that time to study God's word, His truth, and His desire for the world?

I believe He must be grieved over our lack of sensitivity to sin and our gluttonous desire for the guilty pleasures that even the world craves. We look nothing like a holy and set-apart people when we look exactly like the world around us.

A Decluttered Heart

Peter therefore was kept in prison: but prayer was made without ceasing of the church unto God for him. And when Herod would have brought him forth, the same night Peter was sleeping between two soldiers, bound with two chains: and the keepers before the door kept the prison. And, behold, the angel of the Lord came upon him, and a light shined in the prison: and he smote Peter on the side, and raised him up, saying, Arise up quickly. And his chains fell off from his hands. Acts 12:5–7

Does anyone else find this story humorous? I mean, how many of us would be able to sleep in Peter's situation? Yet Peter not only slept but was in such a deep sleep that he had to be hit upside the head to wake up! I just can't even imagine the trust that Peter had in order to be at rest in his circumstances. What a lesson for us! What if we could clear our hearts of anxiety by having that kind of trust in God?

We can also face heart clutter related to stress from finances, our jobs, and our relationships, or really anything that hinders us from completely following the path that God has for us. Passionate pursuit of following Christ requires us to lay aside all that weighs us down.

Now I say, That the heir, as long as he is a child, differeth nothing from a servant, though he be lord of all; But is under tutors and governors until the time appointed of the father. Even so we, when we were children, were in bondage under the elements of the world: But when the fulness of the time was come, God sent forth his Son, made of a woman, made under the law, To redeem them that were under the law, that we might receive the adoption of sons. And because ye are sons, God hath sent forth the Spirit of his Son into your hearts, crying, Abba, Father. Wherefore thou art no more a servant, but a son; and if a son, then an heir of God through Christ. Galatians 4:1–7

Sometimes heart clutter comes in the form of a bitter and complaining spirit. We are dissatisfied with what God has given us and we are craving what we don't have just like the Israelites during the Exodus. The Israelites often complained because they felt like God wasn't going to meet their needs.

And when the people complained, it displeased the LORD: and the LORD heard it; and his anger was kindled; and the fire of the LORD burnt among them, and consumed them that were in the uttermost parts of the camp. Numbers 11:1

Keep thy heart with all diligence; for out of it are the issues of life. Put away from thee a froward mouth, and perverse lips put far from thee. Let thine eyes look right on, and let thine eyelids look straight before thee. Ponder the path of thy feet, and let all thy ways be established. Proverbs 4:23–27

Being Intentional

You are my hiding place; You preserve me from trouble; You surround me with songs of deliverance. Selah. Psalm 32:7

Clutter occurs at all stages and phases. It doesn't matter how much work we have done in the past, how old or young we are, or how long we have lived in our homes. Clutter creeps in when we least expect it, especially if we don't have a system in place to eliminate the excess on a regular basis.

Is your home a haven or a heartache? I mean, is it overwhelmed by chaos and mayhem, or is it a place of refuge and calm? A hiding place from the difficulties of this life? Our own home vacillates between both when things get busy. A deadline, business trip, or heavy sports schedule for a few weeks—each one affects our home. And home can dissolve into chaos when the schedule is relentless. Planning enables me to handle those stressful feelings.

Just as David cried out to the Lord that He was his hiding place, we all need a place of comfort to retreat to when things are busy, difficult, or discouraging. Our homes should be that place of rest for our spouses, our children, our friends, and ourselves. Taking the time to prepare in advance benefits everyone so they still find rest in those in-between moments.

Some of us are natural planners. We have our to-do lists and faithfully check off our duties each day. But we also tend to be the same people who have a freak-out when our routine is disrupted, and our order upended. I can speak honestly about this one because to be perfectly honest, *it's me*!

Others are not natural planners. If you asked them to schedule out their day, month, or year, they'd look at you as if you'd grown antlers and fur. They go with the flow and are always up for an adventure without looking ahead to see if laundry might need to get caught up before you can pack, or if you even have laundry detergent! I can speak honestly about this too because these are the people I live with!

If we plan and live our lives with intention, we can create homes that are a place of refuge for our families, neighbors, friends, and in a larger way, our communities. I'm not saying your home has to be pristine, but a place that is semi-orderly and comforting can relay the message to an overly busy world that they are welcome here. They are wanted, and we can embrace them with love because Jesus loved us that way. Because God is our hiding place, we can create that sense for others as well.

It's not usually a big event that derails us from doing something for the Lord. Many times it's the accumulation over time of a dozen little things. The little things that steal our joy. The little things that spill over into tears of frustration and unkind words. The little things that overflow into our homes from our hearts and threaten to capsize our boats.

The little things like laundry piles after a vacation, a holiday, or a family illness. The dishes piled high in the sink with no help in sight. The paper piles that keep growing with each mail delivery, shopping trip, and homework dump.

This is why it's important to make decluttering a regular habit. We need specific times set aside for removing the excess so that we don't wind up living in a state of overwhelm. To do this, you will need to schedule times to declutter, and you will need to be organized about it.

If you don't already have a system for scheduling your time, here are some ideas: Fly Lady, Stephen Covey, and KonMari each have their pluses. As a young mom, the hourly emails from Fly Lady would help me remember, *oh yes, I do need to move the wash to the dryer. Or, I better defrost some meat now at 11am, or we will eat nothing tonight, or bust the budget for takeout.*

Stephen Covey helped me plan out my day in fifteen-minute increments. I still love this method, honestly. It looks like *so much time* when there are all these empty blocks on my page. Even if I write, "Laundry" in four blocks in a row, it just looks so much more impressive.

Being intentional about scheduling your days will allow you to work in specific times for decluttering.

Another good rule to follow is that for every item you bring in, you must remove one. Keeping up with this ensures that you stay on top of the clutter monsters that threaten to make life miserable.

In general, remind yourself to keep the necessities, toss the broken things, and donate things that others might need or want. As this decluttering occurs, I can guarantee you will feel much happier. The things that are left behind can be displayed, arranged, or stored for

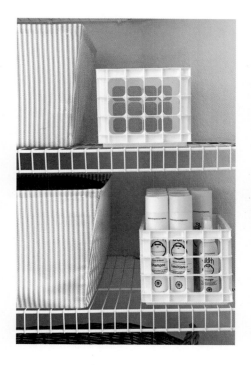

The Main Thing

What does the Lord require of you? To act justly and to love mercy and to walk humbly with your God. Micah 6:8

In design, as in life, we must keep the main thing the main thing. We all struggle to keep our priorities front and center. Staying on task requires living intentionally. Keeping a theme in our home from becoming "eclectic" requires constant assessment and analysis. For each item in a room, consider:

- Does this fit with my aesthetic?
- Does this fit our overall theme?
- Does it provide function and form?

Keeping the main thing in design means not being distracted by every shiny little object. Just as we get too busy in life with too many things, even good things, we can create busy designs that take away from our original design.

In our hearts, we also have to focus on the main thing! The message of the Gospel must be front and center in our thought processes, or we are going to miss the whole point. Our purpose.

A recent discussion with our small group revolved around the question of what keeps us from connecting with God on a daily basis. This group includes people in all walks of life. Several couples have added babies in the last six to twelve months, and you can imagine the answers they might have had.

For many, it was a resounding tiredness, busyness, and lack of time that were the top reasons for not connecting on a daily basis. Many of the couples are just trying to figure out their lives with this new schedule and constant demand on their time. Many of the newly minted moms are trying to go back to work and juggle that added responsibility. Still others blamed it on the lack of routine or failure to plan, being overcommitted because of the struggle to say no, and lastly some were up against the desire to be entertained by sports and movies versus living a life fully committed to chasing Christ.

To live a life without regret when faced with these realities, we must continue to think about where we are placing our treasure. Our treasure is revealed in our priorities and in what we value because we will chase what we love. So we must consistently examine what it is that we love.

> The message of the Gospel must be front and center in our thought processes or we are going to miss the whole point.

later, and the beauty of this process is that everything that remains can have its "place," which makes cleanup much faster and easier. And faster cleanup feels more doable, so you'll do it more often.

The blessing of a faster cleanup is that our homes, once again, become places for people, not stuff!

Choosing Comfort and Care

Many, O LORD my God, are the wonders which You have done, And Your thoughts toward us; There is none to compare with You. Psalm 40:5

When I stop to consider how God cares for me, I am quickly overwhelmed by His great mercy and grace.

His comfort and care exist when my heart is heavy with grief and pain.

His care exists when He provides the next meal even though my budget is broken.

His care exists when a friend texts to say they are thinking about me.

His comfort exists when I can't find it anywhere else.

I can lean on Him to help carry me through. This truth brings great comfort to me and is something I want to share with others.

Making our house a home involves curating comfortable things. A warm blanket, a fresh candle, and soft slippers all comfort us. A room with a quiet nook—a cozy chair, a small table, and a vase of flowers—can be an oasis. But be cautious! Too many candles, tables, or blankets, and the balance is no longer there. Instead, we have created chaos. Creating comfort is not a license for unlimited spending. Rather we should weigh each purchase through the express purpose of making our home more comfortable. Each room becomes an opportunity to invite our family and friends into our space. Some of my favorite conversations with my children through the years have occurred in our bedroom. They will sit on the bed and start talking. If I keep my door open and the space uncluttered, it is much more inviting for them to enter and to unload the day's events, good and bad.

It reminds me of God's love for his children. His door is always open, and he is never too busy to hear from me. His comforts delight my soul and help me pick up my weary head to face a new day. May we offer the same respite in our homes as He has given us.

Seeking Help

The same way we try to hide sin in our lives, many of us try to cover up and mask our clutter problems. We try to hide behind a facade, and it works really well . . . until it doesn't. Emotionally, we will eventually break down under the pressure of trying to keep up the appearances. But we don't need to hide in shame over any state of affairs that we find ourselves in. We must instead learn to be honest, and we may need to say, *I need help.*

I can't do this alone.

I'm overwhelmed and it's making me sad and angry.

When we're honest first with ourselves, and then with each other, we learn that others struggle with the same things we do. Simply knowing that can give you the courage to address the problem head-on.

The thing is that it is risky, isn't it?

Risky that others will find out that we don't have it all together.

Risky that they won't like us once they find out the truth.

Risky that they won't want to stand by us as we seek to fix our dangerous obsession with gathering and gaining more things.

But the reward might be that they don't have it all together either and they find freedom in admitting it, because you did first.

The reward might be that they actually like you better than you thought they did, because you are honest and transparent and not someone to be put on a pedestal.

The reward is they might want to jump in and help find a solution to the problem, and can be a true friend who is honest and able to support us in our time of need.

We won't know until we take the first step.

There is no shame in seeking out those who do this professionally. A professional organizer can sometimes assess our stuff so much better than we can. They have no emotional ties to items, so choosing what stays and what goes is much easier. If this is an expense you can afford and is help that you need—definitely do it!

If the expense is a barrier though, don't be afraid to call a friend and tell them you need help. The essence of discipleship is doing life together, and sometimes to accomplish that we have to learn to be vulnerable and admit we need help. Our friends would be more than willing to lend a couple hours or even a whole day to help us get organized, especially if they knew we needed help. The bonus—the fun that can be had when two friends get to hang out and work together!

Choosing Practical Furniture

I want to talk about the practicality of choosing furniture with an eye toward decluttering and quick cleanup. Units that have storage in them make quick cleanup so much easier! A TV stand that has cabinet doors or drawers can hold games, controllers, movies etc., which helps keep the gear out of sight. Baskets and storage cubes inserted on bookshelves or placed strategically on the floor make great spots to fit papers, art projects, magazines, books, and more.

Being purposeful in your choices of furniture will enable you to manage those quick cleanups when company surprises you or when you don't have a lot of time to do a thorough cleanup.

Practical Decluttering Tips

- **Paper Clutter:** Take fifteen minutes every day and sort the papers! Oh my, they multiply, don't they? Every single day, be ruthless about sorting the paper—that includes mail, school projects, homeschool records, etc. Sort and toss. Anything that you keep must be placed in its folder or box. I have a file for bills to be paid, things to review, and things to file in the cabinet. At the end of fifteen minutes, be done. Feel accomplished and do it again tomorrow.

- **New Purchases:** Every time you bring a new item in the house, whether a new purchase or a gift, remove something. Give it up, friends. Live lean, and then you don't have to clean. Haha! I just made that up. If you don't want to give up anything that is already in your home, then maybe you don't need that purchase after all.

- **Purchase items with dual functions:** Having storage means having the ability to get ready for company quickly. This doesn't necessarily have to come in the form of a closet, though. Plenty of TV stands, entry tables, baskets, and ottomans that are actually hidden storage exist in today's marketplace. Purchasing these items because they have storage is like a gift for those times when you can't see the floor, but you don't have hours to sort and put everything away. Instead, toss everything into those storage spaces, and then the next time you have to stop and clean, spend time sorting and putting the things away in their right spots.

Prepping to Declutter the Whole Home

- Have trash bags and boxes ready to sort your piles for trash/recycle, donate, and sell.
- Limit time in each room. Use a timer to help you stay on task! Make a decision in your sorting and move on. You can revisit it later before you remove the items from your home.
- Keep Post-it Notes or Sharpie markers handy to label the bags and boxes. Especially if you plan to donate or sell.
- Have fun! This doesn't have to be painful.

Two-Week Sample
DECLUTTER PLAN

DAY 1
ENTRANCE

Mud Room
Coat Closet
Baskets
Entryway Table or Storage Spot
Decor/Accessories

DAY 2
KITCHEN

Kitchen Cabinets & Drawers
Pantry
Fridge & Freezer
Kitchen Counters
Cleaning Supplies
Junk Drawers

DAY 3
DINING ROOM

Decor
Linens/Napkins
Flatware & Dishes
Vases

DAY 4
FAMILY ROOM

TV Console/DVDs
Bookshelves
Decor
Pillows/Throws

DAY 5
GUEST ROOM

Closet
Drawers
Nightstand/Side Table

Two-Week Sample
DECLUTTER PLAN

DAY 6

GUEST BATHROOM

Sheets & Towels
Supplies
Drawers/Cabinets
Closets

DAY 7

KIDS/TOY ROOM

Unused Toys
Broken Toys
Drawers
Closet
Under the Bed

DAY 8

MASTER BEDROOM

Closet
Drawers
Nightstand/Side Table

DAY 9

MASTER BATHROOM

Sheets & Towels
Supplies
Drawers/Cabinets
Closets

DAY 10

OFFICE

Filing
Office Supplies
Bills
Paperwork

Two-Week Sample
DECLUTTER PLAN

DAY 11
DIGITAL

Photos
Files
Screenshots
Documents
Receipts
Email

DAY 12
ATTIC/BASEMENT

Old Papers
Decor
Things that haven't been used in a year

DAY 13
CHRISTMAS/HOLIDAY DECOR

Unused or unwanted decor
Broken light strands

DAY 14
GARAGE

Old Papers
Decor
Things that haven't been used In a year
Outdoor Items
Hobby Items
Out-of-Season Clothing

THE END!

Enjoy the Day! You've worked hard!!
Congratulations—I'm so proud of any and all progress you've made!

Decluttering the Whole Home:

1. Have a written plan! Assess each room of your home honestly to determine how much time will be needed. As with any goal, set a deadline to keep the job from lasting forever. The good news is that the more often you declutter, the less time it will take in the future!

2. Sort the stuff, one room at a time. Ideally you will have bins, boxes, or bags to put things in as you sort.

   • If something is trash/recyclable, immediately put it in a trash bag or recycling container.

   • If something is not wanted, decide if it's trash/recyclable or could be donated/sold. Immediately put it in the appropriate pile. The faster a decision can be made, the quicker the process will go.

   • If you are unsure if you want to keep something, set it in the "keep" pile until you are sure you've eliminated all the trash and donation/sell items.

   • Next, go through the keep pile again. Determine if you really need or want everything in it, making sure you have a place for everything that will be kept. Consider if you are keeping the item just because of the memories associated with it. If so, maybe take a quick picture, or write down that memory in a journal, then release it—there's no need to keep it just because of the memories. For items that could be sold, consider the following: Do you have time to either have a garage sale, send items to a consignment shop, or sell on eBay, Facebook Marketplace, or elsewhere? Do you need the money, and would it be a blessing to you or your family? Could you give the money to your church or charitable organization or send someone on a missions trip? If you really have no time, just donate the items. If you have a garage sale and not everything sells, go ahead and donate what's left. Don't bring it back inside!

If you are unsure, ask a few questions:

1. How often do I wear this/use this/etc.? As you sort clothes, remember that you rarely wear all of the items in your closet. Just like we rarely watch all the DVDs, play with all the toys, or use all our kitchen appliances. You want to eliminate the items that you only rarely use. If it's been more than six months since you've used something, you probably can let it go without regret.

2. What value does this item bring to my life today? Most things depreciate, and the value items bring to you today is normally not what you paid for them originally. Is it still adding

value to your life now, or is it something you could give to someone else to enjoy?

3. Can this still be fixed, or is it really junk? If an item is beyond repair, just throw it away. If you won't fix it within the next few months, it's probably not worth hanging on to either. Let someone else take on that project.

4. Do I really love it? No, you don't have to love everything you own, but it's a good idea to be sure you aren't holding on to things just because you feel like you should, or you have to. It's OK to let it go rather than take up space.

Final Thoughts

- If you're really struggling to decide on an item, take the night to sleep on it. See how you feel in the morning!

- Small projects can help build momentum. Cleaning out a junk drawer, a media cabinet, or the stack of magazines/mail can build excitement you need to take on an entire room, and eventually the whole house!

- Take care of your countertops and desk area. Paper clutter can add up quickly to your space, so clear it out and keep it cleaned up. Find a place to keep the papers that must stay and use a one-touch rule to get things put away in the right place each time. The one-touch rule means that at the moment I touch it, I place it where it needs to go. Instead of adding to a pile, I file it in its proper location—in a box or filing cabinet.

Cleaning Tips & Tricks

Don't let the perfect be the enemy of the good. Lower the bar.
Actually spending ten minutes clearing off one shelf is better than fantasizing about spending a weekend cleaning out the basement.[3]

—Gretchen Rubin

Unity, Harmony, and Cleanliness

Now I beseech you, brethren, by the name of our Lord Jesus Christ, that ye all speak the same thing, and that there be no divisions among you; but that ye be perfectly joined together in the same mind and in the same judgment. 1 Corinthians 1:10

Having a home interior that is unified and harmonious requires some planning. A home that feels complete from entrance to exit doesn't just happen. It requires making decisions about what works together and what doesn't, and what the overall goal for each room is. Unity and harmony don't require that each room have the exact same paint scheme or style, but rather that each area of the home works harmoniously together. A home that isn't generally clean is also out of harmony. While a home should be lived in, and not like a museum, a dirty or messy home creates a sense of chaos rather than harmony.

Living in unity and harmony among our family members means that everyone works together to support the same goals, and each pulls their own weight to keep the household running smoothly. Distributing the workload among the household not only takes the pressure off a single person, it also helps us teach our children how to care for their own homes one day.

Hospitality in Scripture

Now it came to pass on the third day, that Esther put on her royal apparel, and stood in the inner court of the king's house, over against the king's house: and the king sat upon his royal throne in the royal house, over against the gate of the house. And it was so, when the king saw Esther the queen standing in the court, that she obtained favour in his sight: and the king held out to Esther the golden sceptre that was in his hand. So Esther drew near, and touched the top of the sceptre. Then said the king unto her, What wilt thou, queen Esther? and what is thy request? it shall be even given thee to the half of the kingdom. And Esther answered, If it seem good unto the king, let the king and Haman come this day unto the banquet that I have prepared for him. Esther 5:1–4

Work Is Messy

Where no oxen are, the crib is clean: but much increase is by the strength of the ox. Proverbs 14:4

We humans are such funny creatures. We long to be pampered and petted but we don't ever want to have to labor. Yet work is vital to experiencing growth and accomplishment. We want to eat the food, but we don't want to have to cook it or clean up from it. We want to live in our homes comfortably, but we don't want to clean it regularly. Then the work builds up and we have to spend all day cleaning on the weekend, or yell at the family to get it together and help.

Proverbs teaches that the only way things stay clean is if there's no animals in the stall. But if there are no animals in the stall, then no work can be done either.

For a few years after moving to Mississippi, our family got involved in the livestock program with 4-H. Can I just tell you, *whew*, those stalls get dirty, my friends. Not a nice kind of dirty, either. We mostly raised sheep, but we added a calf and a goat at one time as well. I cannot imagine cleaning up after an ox! It's smelly, it's gross, and it's backbreaking sometimes. But here's what I know to be true. The kids couldn't go and win medals and earn rewards without

the effort back home. The kids had to feed and clean the animals every day, not just on show days. Not glamorous work, but necessary work. Healthy animals require regular maintenance. Healthy people do, too.

The work they put in, or didn't, always showed up in the arena, and I believe this is true for us as well. Daily and weekly cleaning can become so habitual that they eventually become effortless. Are there times when we get out of the habit and need to do a deep clean or spend a day digging in or even hire some help? Absolutely. Life moves quickly, and sometimes during certain seasons it's impossible to do what we long to do, or long to do well.

But mostly, my friends, I believe that if we set out with purpose and intention to maintain our home, versus cleaning it only when it looks dirty, we would not only enjoy our living spaces so much more for ourselves and for our families, but also would be more inclined to have guests.

Anytime we do work, there is a point where it looks more messy than clean. And as long as we have people living in our homes, our homes will just get messy and dirty again. I mean, we finally get the sparkle and shine on the kitchen counters, only to need to cook dinner. Ugh! It takes one exploding mac and cheese bowl to cover the microwave, a spilled drink in the fridge, or someone walking through the house with muddy boots to wonder why we should clean at all. Honestly, I get it, and I feel that way often, too. Sometimes the daily chores take up so much time, it's all that I get done. This is when I have to figure out how to work smarter, not harder. Spending time working in batches or having a routine that I follow each day, even if it's just a simple one-hour maintenance clean in the morning and before bed, is so much better than spending all weekend cleaning and making the family hate us in the process.

Time spent cleaning is never wasted. The cleaning is necessary to remove the allergens, dust, germs, grime, and junk inevitably tracked in from the outdoors. It is necessary to vacuum, dust, mop, and swipe the glass because without it, the problem just gets worse. Ignoring it doesn't make it go away, rather it increases the amount of time you'll need to devote to it in the future and creates an incredible amount of stress in the process.

Creating Good Habits

One of the most important things you can do each morning is to make your bed. It's not going to clean an entire house, but if at the end of a long day, you walk into your bedroom to start getting ready for the night and see your bed made, you'll feel at least a small sense of accomplishment. Feeling that accomplishment will lead you to want to create more small home-keeping habits in order to feel even more satisfaction and joy in your living space. These small habits will build on each other, and eventually, keeping a clean and tidy home will be routine.

For one week, decide that even if nothing else gets done, you will at least make your bed. Seriously. Once the week has passed and you have firmly established making your bed each day, you can build on it. Perhaps the next thing is to start a load of laundry every morning while your coffee is brewing. Or maybe it's folding the laundry while the kids clear the breakfast table. Truly, staying on top of laundry makes me feel so much more in charge of my life. When it's just a hot mess of piles, I feel as if I can't accomplish anything.

Evening habits are important, too. No one wants to walk into the kitchen in the morning and see piles of dishes waiting to be washed. Taking the time to wash and dry the dishes, run the dishwasher, and wipe down the counters makes the mornings happier and sets you up for more successful behaviors during the day. It's small steps like these implemented over time that become habitual to the point of making you a clean and orderly person. Develop these kinds of daily habits, and you'll see yourself transform into that person that you long to be.

Dividing your year into task lists—daily, weekly, monthly, quarterly, and yearly—can be a great way to create cleaning rhythms. Some tasks will be repeated over and over again, while some may only need to be done once a year.

- Make a list of all the rooms in your home: kitchen, dining room, living room, etc.
- Make a list of all the tasks that need to be done regularly: vacuuming, sweeping, dusting, etc.

Develop these kinds of daily habits, and you'll see yourself transform into that person that you long to be.

- Make a list of all the tasks that happen more occasionally: washing windows, straightening the attic/basement, winterizing your home, etc.
- Now assign a value to each of the tasks: D (daily), W (weekly), M (monthly), Q (quarterly) and Y (yearly).

As you can see some of these tasks are daily, some weekly, and others less frequent. Once you've categorized them as such, then you can create a list of the daily routines. Then create a weekly schedule, and finally note the monthly, quarterly, or yearly tasks on your calendar (see the sample below). Maybe even set a reminder on your phone for those less frequent tasks so you'll know to carve out time for them.

Your cleaning efforts will definitely benefit from handling decluttering prior to cleaning. This will make cleaning go much more quickly!

Sample Cleaning List

Daily Tasks

    Make bed (first thing in the morning)

    Pick up toys

    Laundry: wash, dry, fold, and put away

    Wash dishes and clean counters (at the end of the day)

Weekly Tasks

Monday—Bedroom

    Change sheets

    Dust all surfaces including the fan, door frame

    Clean windows/windowsills/blinds

    Sweep or vacuum

Tuesday—Bathroom

    Clean shower, toilet, sink, and counters

    Clean mirror

    Sweep floor

Wednesday—Living Room/Dining Room

    Dust all surfaces, including light fixtures and fans

    Sweep/vacuum

    Clean windows/windowsills/blinds

Thursday—Front Entrance/Office

    Dust all surfaces

    Sweep/vacuum

    Sort papers

    Clean windows/windowsill/blinds

Friday—Kitchen

    Clean out refrigerator

    Clean counters

    Sweep and mop floors

    Wipe down cabinets

Saturday—enjoy the family or catch up on cleaning as needed

Monthly Tasks

    Wipe and disinfect doorknobs, handles, etc.

    Dust baseboards

    Deep clean kitchen: microwave, oven, vent hood

    Clean trash cans

Quarterly Tasks

    Check the pantry for expired spices

    Check the fridge for expired condiments and dressings

    Wipe down cabinet doors in the kitchen, inside and out

    Wipe out drawers in the kitchen, inside and out

    Vacuum vents and switch out air filters

    Wash blankets, comforters, and decorative pillows/covers

Yearly Tasks

    Rotate mattresses

    Organize basement/attic/garage

    Vacuum and clean vents

    Wipe the walls clean

    Move larger furniture and appliances and sweep under/behind

    Defrost and clean freezer

    Clean light fixtures and lamps

When Should I Hire Help?

I advise my coaching clients all the time that the best use of your time is doing the things only you can do. Sometimes this means that you need to bring someone else in to clean the house. If it fits into your budget and allows you to do the things only you can do, then you should absolutely make that move.

There have been times in our home life where it made sense for us to bring in help. In those seasons it has been such a blessing to allow someone else to take those jobs and let us continue to do other work we needed to get done, participate in family activities, or give ourselves a time of rest.

I think this is so important to consider. Many times we feel guilt for asking and receiving help, but we shouldn't. If it's not financially feasible to get help, then that's when you need to dig in and figure out how to get things done without overloading yourself with work or with debt.

Cleaning Tips & Hacks

Remember when cleaning to always work from top to bottom. When we clean, things fall from the surfaces, no matter how careful we are. Cleaning the floor should be the last step in each room to ensure you're getting rid of all the dust and dirt that's likely to settle as you're cleaning the rest of the room. As you are working through each room, look for items that you can throw in your dishwasher to clean thoroughly and even disinfect. Things like vent grates, toothbrush holders, and soap dishes benefit from a run through the dishwasher. And finish by washing your cleaning utensils, such as sponges and scrub brushes, as well!

Don't forget to keep your cleaning supplies well stocked. There's nothing worse than getting prepped to wash windows and realizing you're out of window cleaner. Take stock of the supplies needed at least once a month and purchase ahead of time. Replace any utensils that are losing bristles or cloths that have too many holes in them. Use a carrying tote or plastic container to keep all of the supplies needed in one place and easily portable from room to room. Preventing yourself from having to run around to get the supplies you need will save you time and energy and will make the process move more quickly. Cleaning doesn't have to be an all-day affair! Here's a list of supplies you'll want to be sure you have:

- all-purpose cleaner
- wood cleaner
- glass cleaner
- microfiber cloth
- additional cleaning cloths
- latex gloves
- small scrub brush
- toothbrush
- squeegee
- vacuum
- mop

Towels
- To get towels really clean, occasionally wash with hot water and a cup of vinegar for one cycle and then a second cycle with ½ cup of baking soda added to the hot water.

Pillows
- Machine wash once a quarter. Add ½ cup baking soda to the wash, along with laundry detergent. To plump pillows back up, dry in dryer with two tennis balls wrapped in socks.

Mattresses
- Use a sifter to sprinkle baking soda on top of the mattress and let sit for about an hour. Vacuum up!

Lampshades
- Try a lint roller to remove dust.

Hard-to-reach corners
- Attach a microfiber cloth to the end of your broom so that you can take advantage of the long handle. The microfiber cloth can grab dust that other rags or sponges cannot.

Ceiling fans
- If you have a telescoping brush and want to dust a ceiling fan, just put an old sheet over your furniture first. If the dust goes flying everywhere, it will land on the sheet, which you can just shake off outside and then toss in the wash.
- If you don't have a telescoping brush, try a pillowcase! Wrap each blade in the pillowcase and as you pull it across the blade, you'll catch the excess dust in the pillowcase.

Dusting
- Used dryer sheets can be used to wipe down surfaces as well—they can pick up excess dust and dirt and then be tossed after use!

Hard-to-remove marks on glass
- A Magic Eraser sponge can remove permanent ink and glue residue off glass. It's also the best tool for cleaning the oven door glass. Wetting one end, you can alternate between cleaning with the wet sponge and buffing with the dry side. It's also fabulous for removing baked-on grease and gunk from your favorite glass casserole dish. A little elbow grease and it's good as new.

Multiuse cleaners

- Dawn dish detergent is a great multiuse cleaner to keep on hand. It gets grease stains out of clothing without damaging the fabric, it helps eliminate clogs from toilets when combined with hot water, and it cleans your dishes by eliminating dirt and baked-on food.
- Hydrogen peroxide and vinegar are inexpensive and useful products for the home. Cleaning glass, countertops, tile, and more, these products can really cut through the dirt quickly and inexpensively. Also, because hydrogen peroxide is a disinfectant, it is great to clean cutting boards and grout.

Meal Planning & Menus

Biblical hospitality is inviting people of all kinds to the table, and creating environments where the gospel, good conversation, and fellowship can be shared.[4]

—Jen Wilkin

No one who shows up unexpectedly expects you to whip up a fancy meal. But having certain go-to snacks and meals in mind and keeping the ingredients on hand can remove some of the anxiety of hosting last-minute guests. Here are some ideas! You can, of course, customize these suggestions to meet your tastes and budget. For example, a simple charcuterie board could consist of just one kind of meat, one cheese, and one kind of dried fruit. Or go all out and create a gorgeous spread! The more you host guests, the more you'll get to know your own hosting style and preferences. Also, try to be sensitive to any food allergies or special diets. If you put a pile of prosciutto in front of a vegan, you'll immediately make them uncomfortable. On the other hand, buying or preparing something special for a guest with gluten intolerance will make them feel welcomed, seen, and cared for.

Charcuterie Board

> Salami
>
> Prosciutto
>
> Hard cheese—cheddar, Parmesan, blue cheese
>
> Medium soft cheese—Gouda, mozzarella
>
> Soft cheese—goat cheese, Brie
>
> Olives
>
> Nuts
>
> Crackers or small sliced toast pieces
>
> Preserves—sweet like apricot or savory like fig
>
> Dried fruits—apricots, figs
>
> Lemonade mix with a pretty pitcher and a special cookie (shortbread or other pre-packaged specialty cookies will keep well on the shelf)
>
> Beverage jar filled with water and fruit. Adding lemon slices, berries, or cucumbers with ice make a beautiful statement without much effort.

Dinner for Small Groups

Potato bar—have everyone bring the toppings, such as bacon bits, sour cream, chives, etc.

Pasta bar—serve a couple different sauces and a variety of pastas. If you like, add a meat such as Italian sausage or meatballs.

Taco bar—have everyone bring the toppings, such as salsa, sour cream, cilantro, lettuce, tomato, etc.

Soup and salad stations—everyone can bring favorite soup, or salad fixings and dressings.

Roast beef sliders/ham sliders—have everyone bring the sides like pasta salad, chips and dip, etc.

Formal Dinners

Lasagna, salad, and bread

Beef roast, potatoes, and carrots

Casseroles—Poppy seed chicken, turkey and stuffing, stuffed shells, chicken enchiladas, etc.

Alfredo Sauce

- ¼ cup heavy cream
- 2 tablespoons butter
- 1–2 cloves garlic
- ½ cup Parmesan cheese
- Salt and pepper to taste

Combine in a saucepan and heat on stovetop over medium heat, stirring until the cheese is fully melted. Serve with fettuccini and top with chicken, or use for a white sauce on pizza.

Seafood Dip

- 1 cup sour cream
- ⅓ cup chili sauce
- ⅓ cup finely chopped onion
- 1 tablespoon horseradish
- 1 cup crab or 15 shrimp, chopped
- ⅓ cup green pepper, finely chopped
- ⅓ cup celery, finely chopped
- 1 tablespoon lemon juice

Combine and chill. Serve with crackers or veggies.

Blue Cheese Spread

- 6 slices cooked bacon, crumbled, divided
- 1 green onion, chopped, divided
- 4 ounces cream cheese softened
- ½ cup sour cream
- 4 ounces crumbled blue cheese
- ⅛ teaspoon cayenne pepper

Reserve 1 tablespoon bacon and 1 teaspoon green onion. Mix remaining ingredients. Refrigerate 1 hour. Sprinkle the reserved bacon and green onion on top. Serve with crackers or veggies.

Homemade BBQ Sauce

- 1 cup sweet onion, chopped
- 2 tablespoons butter
- ½ cup tomato sauce
- 1 cup apple juice
- ¼ cup apple cider vinegar
- 4 tablespoons Worcestershire sauce
- 1 teaspoon hot sauce
- ¼ cup brown sugar, packed
- 2 teaspoons garlic powder

Cook onion in melted butter until they turn clear. Slowly stir in all ingredients, adding brown sugar and garlic powder last. Bring to a boil for about 15 minutes, stirring continuously.

Steakhouse Marinade (for chicken, pork, or steak)

- ⅓ cup steak sauce
- Juice from 1 lime

Combine and pour over the meat.

Asian Citrus Grill

- 1½ tablespoons Dijon mustard
- 1½ tablespoons frozen orange concentrate, thawed
- 1½ tablespoons honey
- 1 teaspoon sesame oil

Combine and pour over the meat.

Covers about 1 pound of pork or chicken.

Pepperoni Pizza Twist

- 1 (3.5-ounce) package pepperoni slices, diced
- 1 (6-ounce) can pitted ripe olives, drained and chopped
- 2 tablespoons snipped fresh parsley
- ½ cup shredded mozzarella cheese
- 2 tablespoons all-purpose flour
- 1 garlic clove, pressed
- 2 packages refrigerated French bread dough
- 1 egg
- 1 teaspoon Italian seasoning mix
- 2 tablespoons grated fresh Parmesan cheese
- 1 (14-ounce) can pizza sauce

Preheat oven to 375°F. Dice pepperoni, chop olives, and combine with parsley, mozzarella, flour, and garlic. Mix well. Place bread dough on a lightly floured surface, seam-side up. Use bread knife to slice each loaf lengthwise end to end, cutting halfway through to center of loaf. Spread open flat. Lightly sprinkle additional flour evenly over dough. Roll dough crosswise to a 4-inch width creating a well down the center of each loaf. Spoon half of the pepperoni mixture down the center of each loaf. Gather up the edges over filling, pinching firmly to seal. Place loaves seam-sides down in an x pattern. Crisscross ends to form a large figure 8. Separate egg. Beat egg white with seasoning mix and lightly brush over the dough. Using bread knife, cut a 3-inch slit in each of the top sections of the twist to reveal filling. Grate Parmesan cheese over loaf and bake for 30 to 32 minutes, or until golden brown. Cool for 10 minutes, then cut. Serve with warm pizza sauce for dipping.

Yield: approximately 16 appetizers.

Veggie Wedges

- 1 (8-ounce) can crescent rolls
- 8 ounces cream cheese, softened
- 1 (1-ounce) package ranch salad dressing mix
- ½ cup mayonnaise
- ½ cup each chopped broccoli, tomatoes, cauliflower, celery, carrots, and green peppers, ham, and shredded cheddar

Spread rolls on a cookie sheet. Prick with fork and bake per directions. Set aside and let cool. Mix cream cheese, mayonnaise, and salad dressing and spread on cooled crust. Mix veggies together and sprinkle on top. Then add the ham and cheese. Make several hours ahead and refrigerate before serving. Cut into squares and serve.

Yield: 16 servings

Deviled Eggs

- 24 hard-boiled eggs, peeled, cut in half with yolks removed
- 1 cup mayonnaise
- 2 tablespoons mustard
- Salt and pepper to taste
- Paprika

Mash yolks with fork until smooth. Add mayonnaise, mustard, and seasoning. Mix well. If too thick, you can add small amounts of water to smooth out dry yolks. Stuff or pipe into egg whites. Sprinkle paprika on top and serve cold.

Egg Salad

- 8 hard-boiled eggs, chopped
- ½ cup mayonnaise
- Salt and pepper to taste
- Dill relish
- Pickle juice

Mix together and serve on your favorite bread or crescent roll.

Yield: 6 servings

Chicken Salad

- Shredded chicken breast
- ½ cup mayonnaise
- ½ teaspoon poultry seasoning
- ½ teaspoon minced garlic
- Salt and pepper to taste

Mix together and serve on your favorite bread or crescent roll.

Yield: 4 servings

Tuna Salad

- 1 can of chunk white tuna in water
- 1 tablespoon pickle relish
- ½ cup mayonnaise
- ½ teaspoon onion powder
- ½ teaspoon minced garlic
- Salt and pepper to taste

Mix together and serve on your favorite bread or crescent roll.

Yield: 4 servings

Spinach Salad

- 1 (5-ounce) package fresh spinach
- 5 bacon strips, cooked and crumbled
- 2 hard-boiled eggs, sliced

Dressing:
- ⅔ cup canola oil
- ¼ cup red wine vinegar
- 2 teaspoons lemon juice
- 2 teaspoons soy sauce
- 1 teaspoon sugar
- 1 teaspoon ground mustard
- ½ teaspoon curry powder
- ½ teaspoon salt
- ½ teaspoon pepper
- ¼ teaspoon garlic powder

Place spinach in a bowl. Combine dressing ingredients in a small bowl. Just before serving, warm dressing mix and pour over spinach. Mix well. Garnish with bacon and eggs.

Yield: 6–8 servings

Wedge Salad

Dressing:

- ½ pound crumbled blue cheese
- ¼ cup sour cream
- ⅓ cup buttermilk
- ½ cup mayonnaise
- ¼ cup red wine vinegar
- 1 tablespoon extra-virgin olive oil
- 1½ tablespoons white sugar
- 1 clove garlic, minced
- Ground black pepper to taste

Salad:

- 1 head iceberg lettuce, cut into 8 wedges
- 2 Roma tomatoes, diced
- 1 small red onion, thinly sliced
- ½ pound crumbled blue cheese

Combine all dressing ingredients and blend using a hand mixer. Place 1 lettuce wedge on each plate. Drizzle equal amounts of dressing over each wedge. Scatter tomatoes, onion, and blue cheese over each salad.

Yield: 8 servings

Blueberry Muffins

- 2 cups all-purpose flour
- ½ cup sugar
- 3 teaspoons baking powder
- 1 teaspoon lemon or orange zest
- ½ teaspoon salt
- 1 cup fresh or frozen blueberries
- ¾ cup milk
- ⅓ cup oil
- 1 egg

Preheat oven to 400°F. Grease bottoms only of 12 muffin cups or line with paper baking cups. In medium bowl, combine flour, sugar, baking powder, lemon zest, and salt. Mix well.

Stir in blueberries. In small bowl, combine milk, oil, and egg. Blend well.

Add liquid ingredients to dry ingredients and stir just until dry ingredients are moistened; do not overmix. Fill muffin cups ⅔ full. Bake at 400°F for 20 to 25 minutes or until light golden brown.

Cool 1 minute. Remove from pan and serve warm.

Yield: 12 muffins

Sausage Balls

- 1 pound sausage, hot or sage
- 2 cups biscuit mix, such as Bisquick
- 1 tablespoon poultry seasoning
- 2 cups sharp cheddar
- 1 tablespoon grated onion

Preheat oven to 400°F. Combine all ingredients, mixing well. Roll into walnut-size balls and place on ungreased baking sheet. Bake for 15 minutes. Drain on paper towel and serve hot.

Yield: 24 balls

Banana Bread

- 2 cups all-purpose flour
- 2 teaspoons baking powder
- 1½ teaspoons baking soda
- ½ teaspoon salt
- ½ cup butter
- ¾ cup sugar
- 2 eggs
- 1 cup mashed ripe bananas (about 2 or 3 bananas)
- 3 tablespoons milk
- 1 teaspoon lemon juice

Preheat oven to 350°F. Grease and flour a loaf pan. Mix dry ingredients. Cream butter and sugar until fluffy. Add eggs, bananas, milk, and lemon juice. Slowly add dry ingredients. Pour into prepared loaf pan. Bake for 55 to 60 minutes.

Yield: 12 servings

Breakfast Casserole

- 1 (5-ounce) box seasoned croutons
- 1 pound sausage
- 4 eggs, beaten
- 2 cups milk
- 1 (10.5-ounce) can cream of mushroom soup
- ¾ teaspoon dry mustard
- 1 (4-ounce) can/jar sliced mushrooms (optional)
- 2 cups sharp cheddar, shredded

Line croutons in bottom of lightly greased 9 x 13-inch pan. Cook sausage until brown, stirring to crumble. Drain well. Spoon sausage over croutons. Beat eggs and remaining ingredients (except cheese), stirring well. Pour egg mixture over sausage. Cover and refrigerate overnight, or at least eight hours.

Remove from the refrigerator and let stand for 30 minutes. Bake for 55 minutes in 350°F oven. Top with cheese and return to oven until cheese melts.

Yield: 6–8 servings

Cheese Stuffed Shells

- 2 eggs
- 2 cups ricotta cheese
- 2 cups shredded mozzarella cheese
- ⅓ cup grated Parmesan cheese
- ¼ cup chopped parsley
- 1 teaspoon oregano
- ½ teaspoon basil
- ½ teaspoon garlic salt
- ¼ teaspoon pepper
- 24 jumbo pasta shells, cooked and drained
- 25 ounces marinara sauce, homemade or store bought

In a medium bowl, beat eggs for 30 seconds, then add ricotta cheese, mozzarella cheese, Parmesan cheese, parsley, oregano, basil, garlic salt, and pepper. Mix until well combined. Fill each shell with ⅓ cup of the cheese mixture. Place filled shells in a 9x13x2-inch pan. Pour marinara over top of the shells. If serving immediately, bake at 350°F for 30 to 35 minutes. Top with a little extra mozzarella if desired and put back in for another 5 minutes or until cheese melts. If freezing, cover tightly and store in freezer. I like to use the foil lids and write the name of the dish and the cooking instructions. Serve with garlic bread and a fresh salad.

Yield: 24 shells, serves 4–6

Slow Cooker Chicken Fajitas

- 1½ pounds chicken breasts
- 2 large bell peppers
- 2 cloves garlic
- Juice of 1 lime
- 1 large onion
- ¼ teaspoon cayenne
- 1 tablespoon chili powder
- 1 teaspoon paprika
- 2 teaspoons cumin
- Tortillas

Combine all ingredients (except tortillas) in a freezer bag and seal. Place in freezer. When ready to use, remove from freezer and run warm water over freezer bag to loosen the items. Dump contents in slow cooker crock and cook on low 6–8 hours. Shred chicken and serve on tortillas. Yield: 6 servings

Hawaiian Pork Chops

- 1 (20-ounce) can pineapple chunks
- 2 tablespoons brown sugar
- 2 tablespoons soy sauce
- 1 pound boneless pork chops

Dump all the ingredients into the bag except the pork. Put the pork into the freezer bag last so that it's the first thing that goes into the crockpot for cooking. To cook, dump the contents of the bag into the crockpot and cook on low 6–8 hours or high for 4–6 hours.

Yield: 4 servings

Florentine Pasta Toss

- 1 (16-ounce) package penne rigate
- 1 (6-ounce) package fresh baby spinach
- 1 teaspoon olive oil
- 2 garlic cloves, pressed
- 1 cup diced red bell pepper
- ½ cup chopped onion
- 1 (15-ounce) jar creamy Alfredo sauce (or see page 88 to make your own)
- ½ cup grated fresh Parmesan cheese plus more for serving
- 2 cups diced cooked chicken
- Salt and pepper to taste

Cook pasta according to the directions. If you are not using precooked chicken but instead need to cook first, save the chicken stock and cook pasta in the stock liquid when done.

Drain and return pasta to stockpot; add spinach. Cover and keep warm.

Heat oil in a sauté pan and add garlic, bell pepper, and onion. Cook and stir for 2 to 3 minutes.

Transfer vegetables and chicken to stockpot.

Add Alfredo sauce to pasta mixture.

Mix well. Grate Parmesan cheese over pasta and mix well again.

Serve with additional Parmesan and salt and pepper to taste.

Yield: 6–8 servings

Chicken & Stuffing Casserole

- 1 (12-ounce) bag bread stuffing
- 1 (10.5-ounce) can cream of mushroom soup
- 1 (10.5-ounce) can cream of celery soup
- 1 whole chicken, boiled and cut in pieces, broth reserved
- 1½ sticks butter
- Sage

Preheat oven to 350°F. Grease casserole dish or 9x13-inch pan. Spread ½ bag of stuffing. Mix soups and broth (about 1 cup) together. Spread chicken on top of stuffing, and then spread soups on top of chicken and top with remaining stuffing. Lay tablespoons of butter across the top. Sprinkle sage to taste. Bake for 30 to 45 minutes or until bubbling.

Yield: 6–8 servings

Pizza-Style Pasta

- 1 pound Italian sausage
- 1 (14½-ounce) can diced tomatoes
- 1 tablespoon dried Italian seasoning
- 1 (16-ounce) package penne rigate, cooked and drained
- 2 cups shredded mozzarella

Preheat oven to 400°F. In nonstick skillet, over high heat, brown sausage for about 8 minutes. Add tomatoes and Italian seasoning and cook for another 2 minutes. Place ½ cooked pasta in rectangular casserole dish. Sprinkle with 1½ cups cheese, then add remaining pasta. Top with tomato mixture and remaining cheese. Bake for 5 minutes. Serve immediately.

Yield: 4–6 servings

Chicken Potpie

- 1 cup chopped celery
- 1 cup chopped onion
- 2 tablespoons butter
- 2¼ cups water, divided
- 1½ cups diced cooked chicken
- 1 cup frozen mixed veggies
- 1 tablespoon chicken bouillon granules
- ¼ teaspoon pepper
- 2 teaspoons cornstarch
- 2 (10-inch) piecrusts

In medium saucepan, sauté celery and onion in butter until tender. Add 2 cups water, chicken, veggies, bouillon, and pepper. Cook uncovered over medium heat for 5 minutes.

Combine cornstarch and remaining ¼ cup water and add to pan. Increase heat to high; cook, stirring constantly, for 2 minutes or until thickened and bubbly. Pour into an ungreased 10-inch pie plate.

Roll out both piecrusts to fit plate; place one in place over filling. Cut several 1-inch slits in the top to vent. Bake at 350°F for 45 to 55 minutes or until lightly browned. Let stand for 5 minutes before serving.

Yield: 6–8 servings

King Ranch Chicken Casserole

- 2 tablespoons butter
- 1 medium onion, chopped
- 1 medium green bell pepper chopped
- 1 garlic clove, pressed
- 1 whole chicken, boiled, deboned, and cut into bite-size pieces. Save broth.
- 1 (10¾-ounce) can cream of mushroom soup
- 1 10¾-ounce) can cream of chicken soup
- 2 (10-ounce) cans diced tomatoes and green chiles, drained
- 1 teaspoon dried oregano
- 1 teaspoon ground cumin
- 1 teaspoon chili sauce
- 3 cups grated sharp cheddar cheese
- 15 (6-inch) corn tortillas, cut into ½-inch strips

Preheat oven to 350°F. Melt butter in a large skillet over medium-high heat. Add onion and sauté for 6 to 7 minutes or until tender. Add pepper and garlic and sauté for 3 to 4 minutes. Stir in reserved ¾ cup broth, soups, diced tomatoes and green chiles, oregano, cumin, and chili sauce. Cook, stirring occasionally, for approximately 8 minutes. Layer half of the chicken meat in a greased baking dish. Top with half of the soup mixture and 1 cup of cheese. Cover with half of the corn tortilla strips. Repeat layers once. Top with remaining cup of cheese and bake for 55 to 60 minutes, or until bubbly. Let stand for 10 minutes before serving.

Yield: 6–8 servings

Chicken Enchiladas

- 1 (10.5-ounce) can cream of chicken soup
- 1 (14.5-ounce) can diced tomatoes with peppers
- 20 fajita-size flour tortillas
- 4 cups chicken, cooked and diced. Reserve stock.
- 3 cups sharp cheddar cheese

Mix soup with diced tomatoes and peppers on stovetop. Preheat oven to 375°F. Take flour tortilla and dip into the stock. Don't leave it in the liquid too long because the tortillas will tear. Just a quick dip. Sprinkle chicken, soup mix, and handful of cheddar into the tortilla and then fold both ends in and wrap. Repeat until casserole dish is full. Pour the remaining soup on top and then sprinkle evenly with the remaining cheddar. Bake until cheese is melted and steaming.

Yield: 6–8 servings

Lasagna

- 1 tablespoon olive oil
- 1 clove garlic
- 1 small white onion
- 1 (16-ounce) can crushed tomatoes
- 1½ teaspoons Italian seasoning
- Salt and freshly ground black pepper
- 1 (16-ounce) package lasagna noodles
- 2 large eggs
- 1 cup mozzarella, plus more for topping
- ½ cup grated Parmesan
- 4 ounces ricotta cheese
- ¼ cup fresh basil leaves, plus extra sprigs for garnish
- 2 tablespoons fresh oregano leaves

Bring a large pot of salted water to a boil for the lasagna noodles.

To make the sauce: Heat olive oil over medium-high heat in a medium saucepan. Sauté garlic and onion until the onion becomes translucent. Add crushed tomatoes, Italian seasoning, and salt and pepper, and stir to combine. Bring to a boil, then reduce heat to low, cover, and simmer for about 20 minutes, checking periodically to make sure the sauce doesn't burn.

Boil the lasagna noodles until al dente, about 15 minutes. Drain and transfer to a large bowl. Toss with olive oil so the noodles don't stick together. Let cool.

Combine the eggs, mozzarella, Parmesan, and ricotta together and set aside. Preheat oven to 350°F. In an oven-safe lasagna dish, spoon a small amount of tomato sauce in the bottom of the casserole dish. Next layer 4 or 5 lasagna noodles lengthwise side by side with edges overlapping. Top with half of the ricotta cheese mixture. Distribute half of the fresh basil and half of the fresh oregano over the cheese, then layer another 4 or 5 lasagna noodles over the cheese in the same fashion as the first layer of noodles. Repeat the process with the noodles and add half the tomato sauce. Add more noodles and the remainder of the cheese mixture followed by the final layer and spread out the remaining noodles, ladle the tomato sauce over, and finish with the remaining mozzarella. Bake in the oven for 30 minutes, remove, and let rest for 10 minutes before slicing. Garnish with fresh basil sprigs.

Yield: 6–8 servings

Elaine Potatoes

- 2 pounds hash browns
- ¼ cup butter, melted
- 1 teaspoon salt
- ¼ teaspoon pepper
- ½ cup chopped onion
- 1 (10.5-ounce) can cream of chicken soup
- 1-pint sour cream
- 10 ounces cheddar, grated
- 1½ cups cornflakes
- ½ cup butter, melted

Heat oven to 350°F. Mix all ingredients except cornflakes and butter in 9x13 pan. Crush cornflakes and mix with melted butter. Spread over top of potato mixture. Bake for 45 minutes.

Yield: 4–6 servings

Creamy Italian Pasta Salad

- 1½ cups pasta twists
- 1 cup mayonnaise
- 1 clove garlic, minced
- 1 teaspoon salt
- ¼ teaspoon black pepper
- 1 teaspoon dried basil
- 2 tablespoons red wine vinegar
- 1 cup quartered cherry tomatoes
- ½ cup chopped green pepper
- ½ cup pitted ripe olives

Cook pasta according to package directions. When done, drain and rinse. In large bowl, combine mayonnaise, garlic, salt, pepper, basil, and red wine vinegar. Stir in pasta, tomatoes, green pepper, and olives. Cover and chill.

Yield: about 6 servings

Summer Squash Casserole

- 4 medium yellow summer squash
- ½ cup chopped onion
- ¼ cup melted butter
- 2 hard-boiled eggs, chopped
- ½ cup shredded cheddar
- ½ cup buttered cracker crumbs

Cook sliced squash in small amount of boiling water for about 10 minutes, or until tender. Drain. Sauté onion in butter until tender. Combine drained squash, sautéed onion, butter, chopped eggs, and cheddar cheese in a 1-quart casserole dish. Top with buttered crumbs. Bake at 350°F for 20 minutes.

Yield: 4–6 servings

Pecan Goody Cups

- ¾ cup butter, softened
- 2 (16-ounce) packages cream cheese, softened
- 2 cups all-purpose flour

Filling:

- 1½ cups packed brown sugar
- 2 eggs
- 1 tablespoon butter, melted
- 48 pecan halves

In a large bowl, beat butter and cream cheese until light and fluffy. Gradually add flour, beating until mixture forms a ball. Cover and refrigerate for 15 minutes. For filling, in a small bowl, combine the brown sugar, eggs, and butter. Roll dough into 1-inch balls. Press onto the bottoms and up the sides of greased miniature muffin cups. Spoon filling into cups; top each with a pecan half. Bake at 350°F for 20 to 25 minutes or until golden brown. Cool for 2 to 3 minutes before removing from pans to wire racks.

Yield: 4 dozen

Snickerdoodles

- ½ cup butter, softened
- 1½ cups + 2 tablespoons sugar, divided
- 2 eggs
- 1 teaspoon vanilla extract
- 2¾ cups all-purpose flour
- ½ teaspoon baking soda
- 1 teaspoon cream of tartar
- 2 teaspoons ground cinnamon

Continued on page 115 . . .

Heat oven to 400°F. In a large bowl, cream butter and 1½ cups sugar until light and fluffy. Beat in eggs and vanilla. Combine the flour, baking soda, and cream of tartar. Gradually add to the creamed mixture and mix well. In a small bowl, combine the cinnamon and remaining 2 tablespoons of sugar.

Shape dough into 1-inch balls; roll in cinnamon sugar. Place 2 inches apart on ungreased baking sheets. Bake for 8 to 10 minutes or until set. Remove to wire racks to cool.

Yield: 4 dozen

Lemon Bars

CRUST

- 2 cups all-purpose flour
- ½ cup powdered sugar
- 1 cup butter, softened

FILLING

- 4 eggs, slightly beaten
- 2 cups sugar
- ¼ cup flour
- 1 teaspoon baking powder
- ¼ cup lemon juice

GLAZE

- 1 cup powdered sugar
- 2 to 3 tablespoons lemon juice

Heat oven to 350°F.

To make the crust: Lightly spoon flour into measuring cup; level off. In large bowl, combine 2 cups flour, ½ cup powdered sugar, and butter at low speed until crumbly. Press mixture evenly in bottom of ungreased 13x9-inch pan. Bake for 20 to 30 minutes or until light golden brown.

Continued on next page . . .

To make the filling: In large bowl, combine eggs, sugar, flour, and baking powder; blend well. Stir in lemon juice. Pour mixture over warm crust. Return to oven and bake 25 to 30 minutes or until top is light golden brown. Cool completely.

To make the glaze: In small bowl, combine powdered sugar and enough lemon juice for desired glaze consistency. Blend until smooth. Drizzle over cooled bars. Cut into bars.

Yield: 36 bars

Forgotten Cookies

- 2 egg whites
- ⅔ cup sugar
- Pinch of salt
- 1 cup chopped pecans
- 1 teaspoon vanilla
- 1 cup chocolate chips

Preheat oven to 350°F. Beat egg whites until foamy. Gradually add sugar and continue beating until stiff. Add salt, pecans, vanilla, and chocolate chips. Mix well. Drop cookies by teaspoonful on ungreased foil-lined pan. Place cookies in oven and immediately turn off. Leave overnight.

Yield: about 4 dozen cookies

Magic Cookie Bars

- ½ cup butter
- 1½ cups graham cracker crumbs
- 1 (14-ounce) can sweetened condensed milk
- 6 ounces semisweet chocolate chips
- 1⅓ cup coconut
- 1 cup chopped nuts

Preheat oven 350°F. In 9x13 pan, melt butter in oven. Sprinkle crumbs over melted butter. Pour milk evenly over crumbs. Top with remaining ingredients and press down. Bake for 25 to 30 minutes or until lightly browned. Cool. Chill if desired or serve warm. Cut into bars.

Yield: 36 bars

Pumpkin Bars

- 7.5 ounces (½ can) pumpkin puree
- 2 eggs
- ½ cup vegetable oil
- ⅓ cup water
- 1½ cups sugar
- 1¾ cups all-purpose flour
- 1 teaspoon baking soda
- ¾ teaspoon salt
- ½ teaspoon cinnamon
- ½ teaspoon nutmeg
- ¼ teaspoon ground cloves
- ⅛ teaspoon ground ginger

Preheat oven to 350°F. Mix together pumpkin, eggs, oil, water, and sugar. Separately, mix dry ingredients. Stir dry ingredients into the wet ingredients and bake for 50 minutes.

Yield: 36 bars

Sour Cream Pound Cake

- 2¾ cups sugar
- 1½ cups butter, softened
- 1 teaspoon vanilla
- 6 eggs
- 3 cups all-purpose flour
- 1 teaspoon orange or lemon zest
- ½ teaspoon baking powder
- ½ teaspoon salt
- 1 cup sour cream

Preheat oven to 350°F. Generously grease and lightly flour a 12-cup fluted tube pan. In large bowl, beat sugar and butter until light and fluffy. Add vanilla and eggs one at a time, beating well after each addition. Lightly spoon flour into measuring cup; level off. In medium bowl, combine flour, orange zest, baking powder, and salt. Add dry ingredients alternately with sour cream, beating well after each addition. Pour batter into prepared pan. Bake for 55 to 65 minutes or until toothpick inserted in center comes out clean. Cool for 15 minutes and then invert onto serving plate. Cool completely and serve.

Yield: 16 servings

Apple Pie

- 6 cups thinly sliced peeled apples
- 2 tablespoons flour
- ¼ teaspoon salt
- ¼ teaspoon allspice
- ¾ cup sugar
- 1 teaspoon cinnamon
- ¼ teaspoon nutmeg
- 1 tablespoon lemon juice
- 2 piecrusts for 9-inch pie (see recipe on page 121)

Continued on page 120 . . .

Preheat oven to 425°F. In a large bowl, toss all ingredients (except piecrusts) together. Place bottom piecrust evenly in pie plate. Pile apple mixture in and then top with crust and slit top. Brush with milk and sugar. Bake for 40 to 45 minutes until golden brown.

Yield: 8 servings

Chocolate Pie

- 2 cups and 12 tablespoons sugar, divided
- ⅔ cup flour
- 6 tablespoons cocoa
- ½ teaspoon salt
- 4 cups milk
- 6 eggs, separated
- 6 tablespoons butter
- 2 teaspoons vanilla
- 1 (9-inch) piecrust, baked

In a saucepan on cold stovetop, whisk together the sugar, flour, cocoa, and salt. Add milk and turn on heat to medium. Add egg yolks one at a time, whisking or stirring after each addition until the mixture thickens (about 2 minutes).

Remove from heat and add butter and vanilla. Let cool and pour into prebaked pie crust.

Beat the 6 egg whites with 12 tablespoons sugar until stiff peaks form. Put the meringue on top and bake in the oven at 350°F–375°F until lightly brown on top.

Yield: 8 servings

Pastry

- 1 cup flour
- ½ teaspoon salt
- ⅓ cup plus 1 tablespoon shortening
- 2 to 3 tablespoons cold water

In a medium bowl, mix together flour and salt. Cut in shortening until particles are the size of small peas. Sprinkle in water, 1 tablespoon at a time, tossing with fork until all flour is moist and pastry almost cleans side of bowl. Gather pastry into a ball. Shape into round on lightly floured cloth-covered board. Wrap in plastic and refrigerate for 15 minutes. Roll out and fit in pie plate.

For prebaked piecrust, bake at 475°F for 8 to 10 minutes.

Yield: 1 9-inch piecrust

Peach Cobbler

- 1¼ cup sugar, divided
- 1 cup self-rising flour
- 1 cup milk
- ½ cup (1 stick) butter, melted
- 2 cups peaches, peeled and sliced

Preheat the oven to 350°F. Combine 1 cup of sugar with flour in a large bowl. Stir in the milk, then the melted butter. Mix until well combined. Pour onto the bottom of a greased 9x13 baking dish. Distribute the peaches throughout the top. Sprinkle remaining sugar over the top, reserving 2 tablespoons for later. Bake for 50 minutes, remove from the oven, and sprinkle remaining 2 tablespoons sugar on top. Bake for 10 minutes, or until the top is golden brown. Serve immediately while hot. Delicious with vanilla ice cream on top!

Yield: 8 servings

Black Magic Cake

- 2 cups sugar
- 1¾ cups all-purpose flour
- ¾ cup cocoa
- 2 teaspoons baking soda
- 1 teaspoon baking powder
- 1 teaspoon salt
- 2 eggs
- 1 cup buttermilk or sour milk
- 1 cup black coffee
- ½ cup vegetable oil
- 1 teaspoon vanilla

Heat oven to 350°F. Grease and flour two 9-inch round baking pans or one 13x9x2-inch baking pan.

Stir together sugar, flour, cocoa, baking soda, baking powder, and salt in large bowl. Add eggs, buttermilk, coffee, oil, and vanilla; beat on medium speed with hand or stand mixer for 2 minutes. Batter will be thin. Pour batter evenly into prepared pans. Bake for 30 to 35 minutes for round pans or 35 to 40 minutes for the rectangular pan, or until toothpick or knife inserted comes out clean. Cool for 10 minutes. Remove from pan to wire rack and cool completely. Frost as desired.

Yield: 10–12 servings

Chocolate Frosting

- ½ cup (1 stick butter), room temperature
- 3 cups powdered sugar
- ¼ cup whole milk, room temperature
- 1 teaspoon vanilla extract
- ⅓ cup semisweet chocolate chips

In a medium bowl, use a hand or stand mixer to beat the butter until light and smooth. Beat in the powdered sugar, milk, and vanilla until smooth and creamy.

Place the chocolate chips in a small bowl and place over a small pan of barely simmering water (double boiler) to heat, stirring occasionally, until the chocolate is melted and smooth (about 2 minutes). Remove the pan from the heat. Add the melted chocolate to the vanilla frosting and store until smooth.

Yield: frosting for one sheet cake

Handy Substitutions:

Self-rising flour—1 cup

Combine:

1 cup all-purpose flour

1 teaspoon baking powder

½ teaspoon salt

Cake flour—1 cup

1 cup sifted all-purpose flour minus 2 tablespoons

Powdered sugar—1 cup

Combine and process in food processor:

1 cup sugar

1 tablespoon cornstarch

Light corn syrup—1 cup

1 cup sugar

¼ cup water

Baking powder—1 teaspoon

¼ teaspoon baking soda

½ teaspoon cream of tartar

Plain yogurt—1 cup

1 cup buttermilk

Buttermilk—1 cup

1 cup milk

1 tablespoon white vinegar

Menu Planning

One of the most freeing things I do for myself and for my family is laying out a few days, a week, or even a month of meals. I sit down and map out several meals, picking our favorites and putting them into a rotation, while adding in a couple of new recipes to try. I then take that number of meals and either duplicate it to extend it for a whole month, or just stick to the schedule I have and create my grocery list. By doing this regularly, I'm able to keep tabs on what I already have in my pantry or refrigerator or what needs to go on the shopping list. When I'm doing *really* well, I'm watching the sales and stocking up on the things that go on sale, and then planning my menu accordingly. Stocking up in this way creates room in our budget because I'm constantly building recipes based on sale items or shopping my own pan-

try when I'm ready to make something else. Even better, when I hear "what's for dinner?" I don't feel annoyed. I have a plan and I know I have the ingredients I need for it. And if I want to invite a guest to stay for dinner, I can either just stretch the recipe a bit further or make a second dish that I had planned for another day. Either way, instead of rushing to the store, I can spend that time with my guests.

Many people resist planning ahead because they think they'll feel pressured to follow the plan perfectly. I have found the opposite to be true. Personally, I find that having a plan is so very freeing. Let's face it, single or married, parent or not, we are all doing a *lot* of things. Having some things figured out ahead of time removes guilt and stress from the equation, and I'm all about that. Here's another thing. If it's Wednesday and I'm supposed to make lasagna but I'm missing a can of tomatoes, or we had a late appointment at the doctor's office because someone is sick, or the car broke down, I don't *have* to make lasagna. I can choose something faster that I had planned for another day. You're not a slave to your plan. Rather, the plan is there to help save you money, time, and energy, so use it as a guide, knowing you can swap things around as life dictates.

When the whole family is involved in the decision making, they are more likely to be excited about mealtime. Ask each family member what they'd like to have one night this week. Depending on your family size you might just have knocked out your whole week! They get excited about the meal they wanted to have, and oftentimes even help with preparing it. I call this a win!

Here's a sampling of our typical meal rotation:

- Mac & cheese
- Spaghetti w/meat sauce (variation: add meatballs or Italian sausage links)
- Chicken & penne with spinach & Alfredo
- Chili
- Tacos
- Taco soup
- Chicken enchiladas
- Homemade pizza
- Hamburgers
- Sloppy joes
- Lasagna
- Spinach lasagna
- Stuffed shells
- Grilled cheese and tomato soup
- Pork tenderloin
- Poppy seed chicken casserole
- Buffalo chicken
- Charcuterie
- Roast beef sliders

Hospitality in Scripture

And it came to pass after a while, that the brook dried up, because there had been no rain in the land. And the word of the LORD came unto him, saying, Arise, get thee to Zarephath, which belongeth to Zidon, and dwell there: behold, I have commanded a widow woman there to sustain thee. So he arose and went to Zarephath. And when he came to the gate of the city, behold, the widow woman was there gathering of sticks: and he called to her, and said, Fetch me, I pray thee, a little water in a vessel, that I may drink. And as she was going to fetch it, he called to her, and said, Bring me, I pray thee, a morsel of bread in thine hand. And she said, As the LORD thy God liveth, I have not a cake, but an handful of meal in a barrel, and a little oil in a cruse: and, behold, I am gathering two sticks, that I may go in and dress it for me and my son, that we may eat it, and die. And Elijah said unto her, Fear not; go and do as thou hast said: but make me thereof a little cake first, and bring it unto me, and after make for thee and for thy son. For thus saith the LORD God of Israel, The barrel of meal shall not waste, neither shall the cruse of oil fail, until the day that the LORD sendeth rain upon the earth. And she went and did according to the saying of Elijah: and she, and he, and her house, did eat many days. And the barrel of meal wasted not, neither did the cruse of oil fail, according to the word of the LORD, which he spake by Elijah. 1 Kings 17:7–16

Start with What You Have

The call to hospitality isn't just for those who have the desire to do it. The call to hospitality is one that is for everyone. But I understand the desire to run and hide. I really do. I love my downtime, my relaxation and my quiet. I thrive on quiet.

But I can't stay here in my comfort zone.

This is not where the best of my life is lived. My life must be beyond myself.

What would occur, my friends, if we took a different view of our homes, our dinner tables, our free time and purposefully, prayerfully, and intentionally used them to make connections with others who need the glorious good news of the gospel?

What if we made gospel outposts out of our homes in order to influence the kingdom through encouraging the saints and winning the lost?

Couldn't we influence someone else's life to look different?

Wouldn't our children behave differently and look differently and see their role in the world differently?

Wouldn't the world look a bit different?

What if we run the great experiment with our resources and laid it all out there? What would God do with our obedience?

God asked Moses what was in his hand and used it. He took the lunch of a young boy and made it expand to feed thousands. Why wouldn't He use us and our resources, too?

We are in a battle for souls, and time is running out. Yet we find ourselves stuck on repeat, making a living and raising our families. And these are good things, but there is more to this life. We need to reevaluate our priorities. If making Him known is our goal, then that should influence every single remaining decision we make—even planning our meals.

What job should I do that will help me make an impact?

What can my family do today that will help me make an impact?

What home should I purchase that will help me make an impact? *(Notice I didn't say that will be comfortable—that's a completely different conversation, isn't it?)*

God doesn't call everyone to have a major platform, speaking to thousands at a time. Most of us are called to make an impact on one person or one family at a time. If we are willing to be obedient for one, God will show us how we can impact more when the time is right to do that.

The house we chose to purchase didn't make sense. After hunting for months across two counties, we only had one home that God opened the door on. We thought it way too big, way too much house, and way too nice. Honestly. That was my conclusion. We walked through and I knew instantly it wasn't right. We didn't need it! We weren't shopping for a forever home, or even the best place we could find. But the reality was this was the *only* home God made

Hospitality in Scripture

I am the rose of Sharon, and the lily of the valleys. As the lily among thorns, so is my love among the daughters. As the apple tree among the trees of the wood, so is my beloved among the sons. I sat down under his shadow with great delight, and his fruit was sweet to my taste. He brought me to the banqueting house, and his banner over me was love. Song of Solomon 2:1–4

available to us in that time. And it is a great home for opening our doors to larger groups. It was a tremendous blessing to be able to purchase this home, and we have always been mindful that we believe God wants us to use it for His purposes and His glory. We've entertained weekly small groups with meals, and we've hosted Christmas parties, baby showers, and more. And here's the thing: we didn't wait to do these things until the kids were old enough to know their manners, our schedules calmed down, or I'd mastered keeping a tidy home. We kept our doors open when the kids were little and interrupted frequently and had sickness, ER visits, and meltdowns. When I felt like a bad mom and a terrible hostess, our doors were open. When I could barely keep the kitchen and living room clean and we closed the doors to every other room, we invited people in. We're not especially gifted in hospitality or unusually selfless or outgoing. We just made a decision and commitment that whatever God blessed us with, we would use whenever He called us to. To be honest, I've done it badly a lot of the time. I haven't always planned meals well. I've burned bread, and I've fussed at my kids. I've gotten stressed out and overwhelmed in the planning and the doing. And yet I always tried to be obedient and tried to keep my heart aligned with God. Sometimes, it was too much and I wanted to run and hide, and yet we just kept serving, imperfectly. And God showed up, being my strength in times of weakness and working things out to His glory, rather than mine.

Once, we were in the middle of hosting our church small group when we got word that there were twenty boys who needed a place for the weekend. The family who had planned to host them fell ill to a stomach bug. It was an easy yes. Not easy in a fleshly sense, but easy when I filtered the decision through the truth that everything belongs to Him, and we desire to always use it for His glory.

Is it inconvenient to host twenty boys for a weekend? Well, sure, kind of. They don't really like to sleep, they definitely want to eat, and, well, showers are a necessity. But we have space, showers, and we can always catch up on sleep. The inconvenience is temporary, and the rewards are, prayerfully, eternal. Who knows what those boys might receive from a weekend focused on Christ?

Just this week another such text came through. The baby shower for Sunday couldn't be held as planned because of the flu. I knew right away that I should offer our house. Not because I had nothing going on. As a matter of fact, I was a week from my deadline for this book and heading out of town for a women's event. But if there is something within my power to do, and God sends out the call, I have to be willing to leverage every resource at my disposal for kingdom work.

When we first moved to Mississippi, I was intimidated by the way ladies hosted events. Southern women do such a lovely job of having the perfect table settings, the most beautiful pottery or china, the loveliest matching cloth napkins. I have often felt like I don't measure up. I have a hard time buying fancy serving pieces or table linens when our regular old everyday ones still get the job done. Yet it's so lovely to go to a home and be treated to nice things. A recent podcast interviewer even shared with me that her mother was a wonderful entertainer in that regard. Her mother had recently passed away and she was fondly remembering how beautiful her mom could deck out a table. She also remembers being afraid her children might break something, and that over time her mom adjusted to accommodate all of them at their different ages and stages.

However, as we attempt to give our best, to make things beautiful and make our guests feel special, let's not set a standard for others that's impossible to attain. I know young people and newlyweds who are afraid to open their homes because they don't have all the serving pieces, or silverware, or even the furniture they think they need. For that I weep. Because that's not what Biblical hospitality is all about. We don't have to have the fine china or best pottery in order to host a dinner party or casual gathering. And maybe those who do it well have

Our hearts matter more than the substance of what we share.

unintentionally sent the message that if you don't have all this stuff, or the room or the tables and chairs, you shouldn't even try.

We don't need to go all out for every event. What if we older ladies (ugh, am I one?) taught our younger ladies that they just need a smile, some disposable plates and napkins, and a hot pizza to share to be warm and inviting and have open doors?

Now please make no mistake—I'm all about the lovely. I really am. I love beauty, and I love seeing those who have a talent for decorating and designing beautiful things rise up and do their thing. But friends, it's not everything. God uses willing hands and willing hearts, whether or not they come with nice couches, beautiful place settings, and gourmet food.

I'm reminded again today that God often blesses us in different ways, during different seasons, for varying tasks. At times, we have an abundance of resources and supplies to open our home easily and bless others. At other times, we may not have much extra to share. But the reality is that it's the heart of it all that matters. We must be careful to always give God and others the best that we can in those moments. Sometimes that's the fancy china and five-course meal, and sometimes it's paper plates and pizza. Either way, our hearts matter more than the substance of what we share. And even if we can afford to host the fancy dinner or party in this season in life, we might be wise to temper the desire to do so now and then. Often the message communicated is that these finer, more expensive things are necessary to do hospitality well, when in fact we each already have what is necessary to open our doors and welcome others in. The resources we have, in whatever season we are in, are all for kingdom work. Paul reminds us in Romans that he knew how to have plenty and to have nothing. That's how we should live our lives, too.

Just start.

Start with what you have.

Share it.

Don't worry about more until it's available.

Then do more.

God always provides what we need when we need it. Just give what you have today and let Him bless it and change it and launch it into service.

What if you took the time to open your doors even once a month? One new family or person, each month for twelve months. I challenge you to try it, and see how God uses your commitment.

Additional Thoughts

To me the essence of hospitality is celebrating people. So every time I have the opportunity to create a place setting for someone, I do it. I feel like it's my way of saying, hello, I see you, I know your name, and I am so, so glad you are here.

—Brandy Bell

Preparing for Overnight Guests

Having a dedicated space for overnight guests is a nicety that some of us have. When this happens, it's so much easier to keep a bed made with fresh linens, etc. But that's not always possible, and it might be that your guest room is also your office, craft room, or even just the couch in your living room! In this case, I like to keep special sheets washed and set aside so that if I need to do a quick change of a bed to prepare for someone last minute, I'm not also scrambling to wash linens.

Having an extra set of towels, a bar of soap, and a fresh candle also makes a quick setup easier for entertaining overnight company. If you have an extra bathroom or one that connects to the guest bedroom, you can set that up with the towels and supplies to be ready all the time.

It helps to keep a checklist of things to do to be ready for overnight guests:

- Fresh sheets
- Pillow
- Comforter/blanket
- Nightlight or lamp
- Place to hang clothes
- Towels and washcloth
- Soap

- Shampoo, Conditioner, Toothbrush, Toothpaste (in case they forget their own). Sample sizes or extras from your last hotel stay work great!
- Toilet paper

When you purchase one of the above items for yourself, grab one extra and set it aside for potential guests. These items don't take up a lot of space and can easily be stored in a drawer or cabinet until needed.

Hygge and Fika

The concept of *hygge* (pronounced Hue-guh) comes from Denmark. The Danish have shown us how to make our homes clean, comfortable, and cozy, and, not surprisingly, it's all the rage. I mean, who doesn't want to come home and crash into a soft bed with cozy blankets, or a sofa with fluffy pillows in front of a warm fire?

To create a feeling of *hygge* in your home, or even in a single room, use all five of your senses.

Touch—soft fabrics and layers of texture, such as pillows, blankets, and throws
Sight—lots of soft muted colors, such as pastels, whites, and grays
Smell—fresh-scented candles, diffuser, or essential oils
Taste—light snacks, easy access to tea/coffee
Sound—soothing and pleasant music. Many times instrumentals fit the bill in a variety of styles including classical, light jazz, or popular and folk tunes.

Does this list trigger some ideas for you? Consider all five senses as you think through how to make a cozy retreat for guests, whether they are traveling for vacation or business, or because they need a place to stay for another reason.

When it comes to bathrooms, you can add some of these same touches in the form of soft towels, a lightly scented candle, and a bar of nice soap. Having these items readily available to guests, whether or not they use them, communicates that they are special and valued. Just like we want to communicate these things to our family, we can take this same principle and apply it to our guests.

If you find this is a huge financial burden and feel like it will hinder you from opening your home, take a step back. You don't have to have all these things to be obedient. You can gather little by little. When you buy one bar of soap for your family, just make it two and store one away for company. You can do the same with toothbrushes, toilet paper—almost any item. Continue saying yes and supply the items you can, while you purchase and pick up new things along the way. Don't say no just because you can't do all the things listed above. These are just ideas for making our places cozy.

Fika is pronounced "fee-ka" and is Swedish, meaning a break in the day for coffee and something sweet. It's a planned and purposeful setting aside of a moment of quality time. Not only would it be beneficial for us to enjoy for ourselves, but it gives us a focused time to invite others over and enjoy time with them.

Flow

The concept of flow can be found in a lot of places. When an interior space has great flow, you likely don't notice. But when passages like hallways or entrances are clogged, it's very noticeable. In discussing the layout of a room and where to place furniture, you want to always keep an eye on doorways and walkways. If you block a doorway, it's no longer usable, so keeping an eye on the flow of the space will affect your choices. As guests come in and out of your home, flow becomes one of the more important considerations of your space. There is always a bit of struggle in trying to find enough seating for everyone without overwhelming a room or blocking the walkway. When guests come in and can move from room to room easily, they feel more comfortable. If you find that you have too much furniture in a room, consider whether you should remove it permanently or take it and store it in another room or the attic.

The front entrance is paramount for good flow. Anyone who has had to maneuver lug-

gage, groceries, or children through a narrow door know the importance of an oversize entryway when it's possible. If a redesign of the door frame isn't possible, it's a great reminder to not crowd that entryway with plants, furniture, or additional items that just get knocked over when we walk in the door. Backpacks, sports equipment, and miscellaneous stuff can make us all feel claustrophobic. In a smaller entranceway, be sure to use neutral colors, mirrors, and good lighting to create a light and airy atmosphere and the illusion of more space.

If you are building or remodeling, opt for stair-free entrances. Creating a level entry enables not only those with luggage to get in the door more easily, it

is also helpful for those with mobility issues. Consider keeping a doormat at the front door for guests to wipe their feet before entering, especially if your flooring gets slick when wet.

Also give attention to lighting choices. Consider how others who don't know your space as well will be able to maneuver through and around your home. Having night-lights, table lamps, and easily accessed light switches makes a difference. On a stairwell, for instance, it will be important to have light switch panels at the bottom and the top, as this will create the safest walkway for everyone.

As you choose flooring for your home, remember that a common material between multiple areas provides the feeling of continuous flow and makes smaller rooms feel larger. Using the same hardwood, tile, or carpet throughout can bring continuity to your space.

Style

Choosing one main style for your home will help it to feel more cohesive. While I can't explore all of the possibilities here, I can highlight a few of the more popular styles you might find today.

- **Minimalist:** simple, refined, and functional. Rooms are kept well edited and most items used must have dual purposes. Generally fabrics don't have prints—they're just one solid color.
- **Contemporary:** generally uses anything that is popular in the moment. It distinguishes itself from modernism because it has more freedom in style. Modernism is known by its boxy, angular look.
- **Traditional:** calm and orderly with classic elements inspired by older European decor. Normally not overdone but more reasonable in scale. Furniture is often centered or paired in a room.

- **Transitional:** a true mix of modern elements with a more traditional base. This style balances warmth and relaxation with unexpected pieces.
- **Rustic:** inspired by the outdoors, combines farmhouse and industrial. Lots of natural finishes like raw wood, stone, and leather.
- **French Country:** a fun hybrid of antique French, shabby chic, and some farmhouse style, too. Mixing the more traditional styles of furniture with more modern prints pulls together the combinations that make this style so enjoyable.
- **Shabby Chic:** rooted in antique and vintage French design, this style has a lived-in and timeless appeal. Soft touches and traditional elements combined with a farmhouse piece or two pull together a real shabby chic feel.
- **Coastal:** known for being light and airy, the vibrant neutrals and coastal colors of blue and green create a relaxed elegance.

- **Hollywood Regency:** An art-deco blend of highly polished glamour. Clean lines with vibrant pops of color combined with crystal, mirror, and highly polished surfaces and finishes. Definitely feels modern and upbeat versus a more traditional style.
- **Scandinavian:** Clean and simple lines create a serene scene. Functional, minimal, and relaxed. A careful balance of elements with lots of tonal texture and lots of white and gray. Colors are hinted in art pieces, pillows, or throws.
- **Bohemian:** a collection of international finds of vintage and antique furnishings. Whether discovered at a local flea market or from actual travels to out-of-the-way locales, this very eclectic style brings glamour to otherwise relaxed decor. And don't forget the houseplants—plants of various varieties and sizes often supplement this decor.
- **Mid-Century Modern:** a style from the 1950s and 1960s that is popular because of its clean, retro, Danish-inspired feel. Simple silhouettes, functionality, and organic shapes are all classic style elements.

- **Industrial:** creating an urban vibe with warehouse/factory elements, whether it's exposed brick, unfinished metals, or filament lightbulbs. Characterized by clean lines and a "hard" aesthetic.
- **Modern Farmhouse:** warm, practical, comfortable, and relaxed. Modern farmhouse is known for its warm and inviting hues with lots of contrasts and rustic country elements.

Having a sense of style and working to understand what things you are drawn to will help you create a more cohesive home as you bring pieces of furniture and accessories in. Without a clear understanding of what works well together, you will struggle to achieve a look you really enjoy.

The really exciting thing is that there is no "wrong" style. We are each unique and different, and our personalities can be reflected in the styles we decorate with. The key is to not overwhelm. Err on the side of simplicity. Almost any style can be seen with appreciation when done well, even if it's not a personal preference.

This reminds me of how the body of Christ looks. We are all unique and individual. There is no one way that is correct, and none of us are exact carbon copies of another. I think that's so valuable for us to remember, don't you? What a boring home, church, community, and world it would be if we all looked, talked, and acted alike. We should look for the beauty and quality of uniqueness in each other just as we can enjoy a variety of styles in our homes.

Form & Function

The age-old debate of form over function or function over form continues on. We all love beautiful things, but sometimes they aren't very practical or the right choice for this season of life. Picking up multiple items that you love as you walk through a department store without considering how all the pieces will work together isn't wise because they will end up becoming part of the clutter problem.

When it comes to interior design, it's always a good idea to have form follow function. Don't fall for the shiny things and fill your space with unimportant items. Create a space that's efficient and appealing. And of course, whenever possible, try to find home furnishings that are both functional and beautiful.

As you determine the functionality of your living space, it's helpful to consider how you want it to be used. Here are some questions you can ask yourself:

- Do I want this space to look fun or formal?
- Who will be using this space?
- How does this room need to function? (office, game room, living room, etc.)

Keep in mind that choices about form that you make today aren't permanent; rather, they can be adjusted during different seasons of your family life. Function, on the other hand, is much harder to change once the walls have been placed! Also consider that those without a plan will inevitably spend more than necessary as they struggle to find the right piece or placement for all their purchases. The financial drain can be devastating.

As your home becomes the central location for family and friends, you can allow your style and taste to influence design—just be sure to keep an eye on the functionality first. This might mean purposing for dual-purpose rooms with multiuse furniture.

Living Rooms—Consider how many will be watching TV. Make sure you have enough seats to all sit together at one time. Floor seating like poufs or oversize pillows and smaller chairs that can be moved easily to other rooms when not needed are ideal. Cabinets or armoires can hold children's items on the bottom with adult components and accessories on higher levels out of the reach of little fingers.

Kitchen—How much cooking will you be doing? Do you need to keep an eye on the kids doing homework while you are making breakfast or dinner? Do you have room for an island,

or is it more efficient to keep the space free for several people to work in the kitchen at the same time?

I certainly believe in the value of lots of countertop space. Having space to work makes the process so much easier.

Bathrooms—Does the whole family share a bathroom? Then having different drawers or containers for each person might work best. Try for as much storage potential as possible.

Bedrooms—Bedrooms should be relaxing and peaceful. Lots of texture and softness make the space inviting while we sit quietly to work, read for fun, or just unwind at the end of a long day.

Multiuse Rooms—Add extra dining space by utilizing a dropleaf table. When not being used for dining, it can double as a console table. A home office that has a sofa bed or futon can double as a guest room.

Once you've decided your room's function, focus on how you want it to feel. Small gestures such as extra pillows, a soft throw, or a scented candle all add to the mood of the room and the coziness that we all crave.

Cross-Cultural Hospitality

It's important to remember that other cultures do meals and hospitality in their homes in different ways. When you invite others in, try to learn about their culture and be willing to make some accommodations.

I have a friend who was a missionary in India for several years. She learned early on that wives were to be seen but not present during the meals. She learned that over time they could become more casual in their interactions and she could join for meals, but in the beginning it was important to honor the culture they were in by following the written and unwritten rules.

Another thing she learned was that the order of hospitality was unlike American traditions. We tend to come in, sit down and eat, and then stay and visit after. In India they would visit first and end with the meal. Once they ate, they would leave. This is important information, isn't it? Hurt feelings or awkwardness can occur if we aren't sensitive to or aware of cultural differences.

Being willing to practice cross-cultural hospitality means accepting that we will make mistakes. We can either wait until we know all we are supposed to know before we act and reach out to others, or we can learn along the way as we come in a spirit of humility and love.

> We can either wait until we know all we are supposed to know before we act and reach out to others or we can learn along the way as we come in a spirit of humility and love.

Modeling Hospitality

Teaching our children to be hospitable means modeling hospitality for them early and often. We want them to understand the nature of the sacrifice of hospitality but also the true joy it brings us when we encourage and inspire those in need because we give of our lives, our homes, and our resources.

We have to begin with teaching our children to see the needs of those around them. Perhaps this means taking them with you when you drop off a meal to a family that has experienced a birth or a death. It might mean bringing them to visit a shut-in at the nursing home. Maybe it's modeling how they should give up their bed for a short time for someone else to be comfortable and cared for. The more we encourage them to work through these inconveniences, the more willing they will be to choose to see those needs in the future and be willing to act first in those circumstances.

When our hearts are in the right place, we remember that our guests are at the center of the things we choose to do. From picking their favorite meal, to watching their favorite show or playing games around the table, teaching children to put others first is such a beautiful lesson.

Philippians 2:3 Let nothing be done through strife or vainglory, but in lowliness of mind let each esteem other better than themselves.

I believe it's also important to involve our children in the planning of when to have guests over. Pulling out the calendar and blocking off a time for a visit or even a meal shows them how to plan ahead and decide in advance to be willing to open their hearts and their doors. Learning to sacrifice in a small way to put others ahead of themselves is a life lesson that will have long-term effects.

Biblical Hospitality Is Counterculture

To be ready to influence the world, our inward parts must be ready and aligned with Christ. Seeing others the way God sees them is the prayer of my heart. But I have to ask myself often, "What does the gospel mean to me personally? Has it changed me? Do I look different?"

Consistent assessment of the battles I am facing in my heart will help propel me forward. What am I battling within my heart that is prohibiting me from being fully ready to follow Christ? This is the clutter. We must remove it to be ready to move forward. And we must be ready to move forward in order to walk out the obedience Christ has called us to.

We will never be perfect, but we are called to be different. One way we demonstrate this difference is the audacity with which we decide to be vulnerable. Living in a society today that tells us that we must be more, do more, and project a level of success beyond reality means that to do anything different is audacious. We acknowledge our weakness and vulnerability with one another as we encourage each other. There is something especially endearing and wonderful when we look at someone else and admit that we don't have it all together. In that moment, we allow others to also be honest and to find that many of us are more alike than we are different.

When I choose instead to keep up the walls that divide me from people, I am pursuing my own selfish agenda. This is truly disobedience and comes from a lack of humility. My personal disobedience will not only affect my usefulness for the kingdom, but it can also have damaging consequences for my family. So many times we believe our sin only affects ourselves. "We aren't hurting anyone," we think, but this is simply not true.

Do I stress and worry, or leave a string of chaos behind me, or am I a calming, peaceful presence?

Do I get angry over the smallest inconveniences and mistakes?

Do I give grace and understanding?

What is my attitude toward my home? Complaining and ungrateful or filled with joy and peace?

But the fruit of the Spirit is love, joy, peace, longsuffering, gentleness, goodness, faith, Meekness, temperance: against such there is no law. Galatians 5:22–23

I love Galatians 5:16, too. *This I say then, Walk in the Spirit, and ye shall not fulfil the lust of the flesh.*

The present tense imperative "walk" indicates that this is a choice. I will choose to consistently let the Spirit of God have control over my "manner of living." In order to be willing to choose this way of life, I must be consistently studying God's word and applying it to my heart. God got my attention several years ago and made it very clear to me that in order to continue passionately pursuing Him and his agenda, I needed to become a committed believer. My walk was too inconsistent, and it was time to break the habits that I had allowed to take root in my life. When God was directing my path into writing and speaking, it was preceded by the decision to wake early to guarantee a consistent quiet time each morning. Getting up early was a drastic move, but after years of avoiding the responsibility I knew I was avoiding, God opened doors and moved me forward into expanded and new service areas. But I had to be willing to walk in faith and follow the path God had for me.

I wonder if you might be prompted today to think about your own service. Could you do more for the kingdom with whatever resources God has blessed you with? What could you leverage in your life to make biblical hospitality a habit? Who could benefit from your love and the living out of the gospel in your daily life?

The story of Esther reminds me that if God places us in a comfortable spot, it's probably not just to relax. The palace was not Esther's calling. Rescuing God's people was her calling. The palace was just the vehicle to help her accomplish her calling.

In Our Community and the World

And a certain woman named Lydia, a seller of purple, of the city of Thyatira, which worshipped God, heard us: whose heart the Lord opened, that she attended unto the things which were spoken of Paul. And when she was baptized, and her household, she besought us, saying, If ye have judged me to be faithful to the Lord, come into my house, and abide there. And she constrained us. Acts 16:14–15

Lydia is a great example of someone who understood the importance of biblical hospitality. As soon as she became a Christ follower she turned around and opened her home to those who had a need.

When my heart and home are in proper alignment, I can then be ready for God's assignment!

To miss a kingdom assignment because we've become too caught up in our personal kingdom is one of the greatest tragedies we could ever face.

God has given each of us a job, position, resources, education, and more. God has opened opportunities to optimize His kingdom purposes. He didn't place you or me where we are so we could eat figs all day long or post pictures on social media. He's placed us wherever we are because we are in the midst of a battle, a war. You and I are in the midst of a seismic conflict involving good versus evil.

To miss a kingdom assignment because we've become too caught up in our personal kingdom is one of the greatest tragedies we could ever face. An entire nation was grateful for how Esther responded to Mordecai's rebuke. Their lives were spared. How many souls can be spared in the culture where we live today when we choose to step up to service, even if it involves sacrifice?

Look carefully then how you walk, not as unwise but as wise, making the best use of the time, because the days are evil. Ephesians 5:15–16

Jesus loved people, and if I am going to reflect Jesus to others, I must love people, too. Showing love might mean different things at different times, but I'm sure it often means bringing people into my space. Sometimes that means bringing them into our messes, but mostly it means being comfortable with the role Christ calls us to and utilizing all the blessings He has given us for kingdom work.

Endnotes

1 Christopherson, Jeff. "The Power of Biblical Hospitality." *The Exchange* https://www
.christianitytoday.com/edstetzer/2019/august/power-of-biblical-hospitality-entertainment
-jesus.html.

2 Scalise, Christina. *Organize Your Life and More: Save Time and Money, Reduce Stress, Remove Clutter.* Chandler, AZ: Brighton Publishing LLC, 2012.

3 "Overwhelmed? 9 Quick Tips for Keeping Your Home Feeling Serene and Organized." Gretchen Rubin. Accessed February 4, 2020. https://gretchenrubin.com/2012/03/feeling
-overwhelmed-tips-to-keep-your-life-feeling-serene-and-under-control-be-wary-of
-bargains-or-sales-do-you-re/.

4 Wilkin, Jen. "What's the Difference Between Hospitality and Entertaining?" The Gospel Coalition, December 22, 2017. https://www.thegospelcoalition.org/video/whats
-difference-hospitality-entertaining/.

Photography Credits

Special thanks to these contributors for sharing their amazing perspectives in visual and written form:

Arianne Miller, @millhousestyle

Brandy Bell, @sobellandco / www.sobellandco.com

Caroline Bivens, @c.b._designs / www.carolinebivensdesigns.com

Jennifer Ingram, @graciousspaces / www.gracious-spaces.net

Julie Paisley Photography, @juliepaisley / www.juliepaisley.com

Justin Fox Burks Photography, @justinfoxburks / www.justinfoxburks.com

Kathy Atkins, @beautifullyadorned / www.livebeautifullyadorned.com

Kelly Radcliff, @thetatteredpew / www.thetatteredpew.com

Paige Rien, @paigerien/ www.paigerien.com

Pamela Saumure, @pamela.saumure

Sarah Symonds, @graceinmyspace/www.graceinmyspace.com